T0002864

100 WORDS

ALMOST

everyone

MISPRONOUNCES

THE **100** WORDS® *From the Editors of the*
AMERICAN HERITAGE®
DICTIONARIES

HOUGHTON MIFFLIN HARCOURT

Boston   New York

THE 100 WORDS® is a registered trademark of
Houghton Mifflin Harcourt Publishing Company.

Visit our websites: ahdictionary.com
and hmhbooks.com

LIBRARY OF CONGRESS CATALOGING-IN-PUBLICATION DATA

100 words almost everyone mispronounces / from the editors of the American
Heritage dictionaries.
    p. cm. -- (The 100 words)
  Includes index.
  ISBN-13: 978-0-547-14811-3
  ISBN-10: 0-547-14811-9
1. English language--Pronunciation--Dictionaries. 2. English language--Usage--
Dictionaries. I. Title: One hundred words almost everyone mispronounces.
  PE1137.A15 2008
  421'.5203--dc22

                        2008025672

Text design by Anne Chalmers

MANUFACTURED IN THE UNITED STATES OF AMERICA

2 3 4 5 - EB - 15 14 13 12

Table of Contents

100 Words
Almost Everyone
Mispronounces

The 100 Words

Preface

100 Words Almost Everyone Mispronounces takes its place as the ninth book in the best-selling 100 Words series. These books provide a detailed look at expressive and important words we all should know as effective communicators.

But to use words effectively it helps to know how to pronounce them, or at least how not to mispronounce them.

Determining when a word is mispronounced is not always easy. As a part of human culture, language is always changing, and if anything, this book shows that many of today's correct pronunciations were yesterday's mistakes. The alterations have become acceptable because they became so widely used that to object to them would seem peculiar. The mistake, the unwarranted change in sound, became the norm. How?

Many words that have troubled pronunciations are more often seen than heard. That is, we encounter them more often in reading than in conversation, and when we do have occasion to use them in speech, we find ourselves guessing at the proper way to say them. Which syllable should be stressed most strongly in the words *desultory* and *plethora*?

Many English words are borrowed from other languages, and it is normal for borrowings to be made more like existing English words in a process called Anglicization. A powerful engine for pronunciation change is the desire to fit words into regular and familiar patterns, and so to model new or unusual words after existing ones. For instance, the word *debacle*, borrowed from French, is being Anglicized along the model of other *–cle* words like *spectacle* and *miracle*. The word *portentous* is sometimes pronounced as if it were spelled "portentious," along the model of *pretentious* and other *–tious* words. "Portentious" we might rightly consider a mistake, but *debacle* rhyming with *spectacle* seems a legitimate Anglicization.

What language the word comes from, when it was borrowed, how it fits into the existing sound patterns of English—all of these factors have some influence on its current sound. Quite often the various tendencies compete with each other, and people use more than one pronunciation. Many people pronounce the word *cadre* as if it ended in *–ay*, even though the original French word did not have this sound. But people do this by analogy with other French borrowings that do have the *–ay* sound, like *cachet*, even when it's unwarranted. Think *lingerie*.

Clearly one of the chief reasons we change the way we pronounce words is to make the words easier to say. This process does not just involve Anglicizing difficult foreign borrowings, but simplifying the native sounds of English as well, especially in clusters of consonants. This is why we don't pronounce the *b* in *climb,* for example, or the *d* in *handkerchief*. Competing against this tendency is a desire to pronounce words as we see them spelled. Sometimes sounds that have dropped out are restored, as is the case with the *n* sound in *kiln* and the *t* sound in *often*.

Reasons like these explain how some erroneous pronunciations have arisen. But for others, a great deal of mystery remains. Why should *harass* have developed stress on a different syllable? Why should *flaccid* develop a new pronunciation "flassid" beside the older "flaksid," when no one pronounces *vaccine* as "vassine"? Did a new pronunciation begin when a few children misheard a word and continued to pronounce it that way, until their mispronunciation spread to others? For many words, no one knows.

But we still have to ask ourselves: Which pronunciation is acceptable? Will I sound foolish saying the word this way?

Don't be foolish. Read further and find out.

— Joseph Pickett,
Executive Editor

Guide to the Entries

ENTRY WORDS The 100 words in this book are listed alphabetically. Each boldface entry word is followed by its pronunciation (see page ix for a pronunciation key) and at least one part of speech. One or more definitions are given for each part of speech with the central and most commonly sought sense first.

ETYMOLOGIES (WORD HISTORIES) Etymologies appear in square brackets following the quotations. An etymology traces the history of a word as far back in time as can be determined with reasonable certainty. The stage most closely preceding Modern English is given first, with each earlier stage following in sequence. A language name, linguistic form (in italics), and brief definition of the form are given for each stage of the derivation presented. For reasons of space, the etymologies sometimes omit certain stages in the derivation of words with long and complex histories, whenever this omission does not significantly detract from a broad understanding of the word's history. To avoid redundancy, a language, form, or definition is not repeated if it is identical to the corresponding item in the immediately preceding stage. The word *from* is used to indicate origin of any kind: by inheritance, borrowing, abbreviation, the addition of affixes, or any other linguistic process. When an etymology splits a compound word into parts, a colon comes after the compound word, and the parts (along with their histories in parentheses) follow in sequence linked by plus signs (+). Occasionally, a form will be given that is not actually preserved in written documents, but that scholars are confident did exist — such a form will be marked by an asterisk (*).

Pronunciation Guide

Pronunciations appear in parentheses after boldface entry words. If a word has more than one pronunciation, the first pronunciation is usually more common than the other, but often they are equally common. Pronunciations are shown after inflections and related words where necessary.

Stress is the relative degree of emphasis that a word's syllables are spoken with. An unmarked syllable has the weakest stress in the word. The strongest, or primary, stress is indicated with a bold mark (ʹ). A lighter mark (ʹ) indicates a secondary level of stress. The stress mark follows the syllable it applies to. Words of one syllable have no stress mark because there is no other stress level that the syllable can be compared to.

The key on page ix shows the pronunciation symbols used in this book. To the right of the symbols are words that show how the symbols are pronounced. The letters whose sound corresponds to the symbols are shown in boldface.

The symbol (ə) is called *schwa*. It represents a vowel with the weakest level of stress in a word. The schwa sound varies slightly according to the vowel it represents or the sounds around it:

a·bun·dant (ə-bŭnʹdənt)   **mo·ment** (mōʹmənt)

civ·il (sĭvʹəl)   **grate·ful** (grātʹfəl)

PRONUNCIATION KEY

Symbol	Examples	Symbol	Examples
ă	pat	oi	noise
ā	pay	o͝o	took
âr	care	o͝or	lure
ä	father	o͞o	boot
b	bib	ou	out
ch	church	œ	*German* schön
d	deed, milled	p	pop
ĕ	pet	r	roar
ē	bee	s	sauce
f	fife, phase,	sh	ship, dish
	rough	t	tight, stopped
g	gag	th	thin
h	hat	*th*	this
hw	which	ŭ	cut
ĭ	pit	ûr	urge, term,
ī	pie, by		firm, word,
îr	deer, pier		heard
j	judge	v	valve
k	kick, cat, pique	w	with
KH	*Scottish* loch	y	yes
l	lid, needle	z	zebra, xylem
m	mum	zh	vision,
n	no, sudden		pleasure,
N	*French* bon		garage
ng	thing	ə	about, item,
ŏ	pot		edible, gallop,
ō	toe		circus
ô	caught, paw	ər	butter
ôr	core		

Whether you say "ACK-you-min" or "a-CUE-min," it is no reflection on your linguistic **acumen**. Both pronunciations are acceptable—although nowadays "ACK-you-min" is heard much more than "a-CUE-min."

(1)

acumen (ăk′yə-mən, ə-kyōō′mən)

noun

Quickness, accuracy, and keenness of judgment or insight: *"Rock-and-roll has become a job opportunity for younger people not otherwise gifted with business acumen"* (Rick Moody, "Against Cool," *Gingko Tree Review*).

℘ *Acumen* has been in English since the 16th century, and the pronunciation (ə-kyōō′mən), with stress on the second syllable, is the traditional pronunciation reflecting the word's Latin origin. In the middle of the 20th century a pronunciation with stress on the first syllable, (ăk′yə-mən), arose and in time began displacing the original. Both pronunciations are correct nonetheless. The shifting of stress onto the first syllable is a hallmark of the Anglicization of foreign words in English, also seen in the words *debacle* and *victuals.*

[Latin *acūmen*, from *acuere*, to sharpen, from *acus*, needle.]

aegis (ē'jĭs)

noun

1. Protection: *a child whose welfare is under the aegis of the courts.* **2.** Sponsorship, patronage, or support: *"He resumed teaching two of his courses under the aegis of the combined languages and literature program"* (Philip Roth, *The Human Stain*). **3.** Guidance, direction, or control: *"the Mamelukes, the warrior caste that ruled Egypt under the distant aegis of the Turkish sultan"* (David A. Bell, *The First Total War*). **4.** *Greek Mythology* The goatskin shield or breastplate of Zeus or Athena. Athena's shield carried at its center the head of Medusa.

❧ The *ae* vowel cluster is relatively rare in English. Unfortunately for the student of English pronunciation, it can represent a wide variety of sounds. For instance, the *aer–* in *aerate* is pronounced (âr) like *air*, but the *caer–* in *caerphilly* is pronounced (kär) like *car*. The *Caed–* in the name of the Old English poet Caedmon is pronounced (kăd) like *cad*, but the *–phaes–* in the name of the Greek god *Hephaestus* can be pronounced (fĕs) as in *confess* or (fēs) like *feast* without the *t*. The *tae* of *tae kwon do* (a word borrowed from Korean) is also pronounced like *tie*. But in words like *Kafkaesque* and names like *Laertes* the *–ae–* is split between two separate syllables.

So predicting how to pronounce words that have the *ae* cluster is difficult, to say the least. Nonetheless, in the greatest number of cases, especially in words originating in Greek and Latin, *ae* is normally pronounced in English as (ē). In fact, many of these words are often spelled in English with a simple *e* in place of the *ae*; thus *aegis, aeon, caesarian, mediaeval,* and *Praetorian* are also spelled *egis, eon, cesarian, medieval,* and *Pretorian*.

[Latin, from Greek *aigis*, goatskin, skin shield, aegis, from *aix, aig-*, goat.]

affluent (ăf′loō-ənt, ə-floō′ənt)

adjective

Generously supplied with money, property, or possessions; prosperous or rich.

☙ *Affluent* has been in the English vocabulary since medieval times. It comes from the Latin present participle *affluens*, by way of Old French. Traditionally, *affluent* has been stressed on the first syllable, and it shares the stress pattern of similar three-syllable words like *arrogant* and *eloquent* that also come from Latin present participles.

The pronunciation (ə-floō′ənt), with stress on the second syllable, is an innovation of the last half of the 20th century and did not show up in most dictionaries until the 1980s. This pronunciation has become widespread and cannot be considered a mistake, although it tends to grate upon the ears of traditionalists. *Congruent* is another word like *affluent* that has traditionally been stressed on the first syllable but is now often stressed on the second. The related nouns *affluence* and *congruence* have similar pronunciation variants.

[Middle English, abundant, flowing, from Old French, from Latin *affluēns, affluent-*, present participle of *affluere*, to abound in : *ad-*, toward, to + *fluere*, to flow.]

almond (ä′mənd, äl′mənd , ôl′mənd, ăm′ənd)

noun

1. A deciduous tree (*Prunus dulcis*), native to Asia and northern Africa and having alternate, simple leaves, pink flowers, and leathery fruits. **2.** The ellipsoidal kernel of this tree, either eaten as a nut or used for extraction of an oil for flavoring.

The almond is a common nut, but it goes by many pronunciations. First, there is the question of how the vowel in the first syllable should sound. Then there is the question of whether the *l* should be pronounced or not. And then there is the question of which combination to use: which vowel, plus or minus *l*? Luckily, all of these combinations are considered acceptable in contemporary English.

Lovers of the *l* will be comforted to know that *almond* has had an *l* in English from the start, from around 1300, at least in spelling, as it had in its Old French source, *almande*. The Old French word developed from Classical Latin *amygdala,* and the Latin word is a borrowing of Greek *amugdale.* (Recall that the amygdala is the "almond-shaped" organ in the brain.)

The written *l* may have been introduced by way of the Spanish word for "almond," *almendra,* which also comes from Latin *amygdala.* It is not surprising that Spanish may have had an influence on the English word for "almond," since Spain has long been a major producer of the nuts. The *l* in the Spanish word may reflect the influence of the many other nouns in Spanish beginning with the letters *al–,* like *albañil,* "mason," *albóndiga,* "meatball," *alfombra,* "carpet," *algodón,* "cotton," and *almohada,* "pillow." Most of these nouns beginning with *al–* were borrowed from Arabic. When Spanish borrowed nouns from Arabic words, they borrowed them with the Arabic definite article *al,* "the," tacked on to the beginning. For instance, Spanish *alfombra,* "carpet," comes from Arabic *al-ḥanbal,* "the carpet." A trace of the Arabic article *al* is also found in English words of Arabic origin beginning with *al–,* like *alcove* and *algebra.*

But English speakers began to drop the (l) from pronunciation in the 1500s, when the consonant disappeared in many words before the sounds (f), (v), (k), (m), and (n). This may seem strange, but simplification of consonant clusters is a fairly common phenomenon, and has led to other sounds disappearing from English, such as the (d) in *handkerchief*. For this reason, most English speakers don't say (l) in *half* and *calves, walk* and *talk,* and (usually) *calm* and *palm*, and *almond.*

But in some words speakers began to restore the (l) before (m) as a spelling pronunciation back in the 1700s, and perhaps even earlier. Why this is so is a bit of a mystery since it did not happen in other words like *talk* and *half.*

As for the vowel in the first syllable, it has its own complications. Many people have a broad *ah* sound, like that in *doll*, whether the *l* is pronounced or not. But some speakers pronounce the word as a near rhyme to *jammin'*, with the vowel of *jam*. This pronunciation is a dialectal variant but is not stigmatized. Still others say the word as if the first syllable rhymed with *fall* and *awl.*

To keep it simple: if you want to honor the oldest tradition, you will certainly have plenty of speakers at your side. Drop the *l* and open wide and say (ä′mənd). *Almond, calm*, and their associates are not the only words in English that have had an (l) inserted by way of a spelling pronunciation. From the 1400s on, scholars added a written *l* to words like *fault* (from Old French *faute*) and *assault* (from Old French *asaut*) on the assumption that because the *l* was present in the ultimate Latin sources of these words (*fallere, assultus*), it ought to be in English too. It sometimes took centuries, but eventually English speakers took this lesson to heart, and the old way of pronouncing these words without *l* was forgotten.

[Middle English *almande,* from Old French, from Late Latin *amandula,* alteration of Latin *amygdala,* from Greek *amugdalē.*]

5

antipodes (ăn-tĭp′ə-dēz′)

plural noun

Any two places or regions that are on diametrically opposite sides of the earth.

༄ The prefix *anti–* is most commonly pronounced with stress on the first syllable, as in the words *antibody, anticlimax, antifreeze,* and *antisocial.* One might assume, therefore, that *antipodes* is pronounced (ăn′tĭ-pōdz) with the prefix *anti–* pronounced in the same way. But the stressing of *anti–* on the first syllable is not a universal rule, especially when the prefix is not combined with a preexisting English word. In cases where the *anti–* was prefixed to a Greek or Latin root before the word was adopted into English, the stress is more often on the second syllable, as in *anticipate, antipathy,* and *antiphonal.* Such is also the case with *antipodes.*

As for the *–podes* of *antipodes,* you may well suppose that *antipodes* represents a straightforward plural form of a singular *"antipode,"* in the same way that *episodes* is the plural of *episode* and *diodes* is the plural of *diode.* Such a supposition, however justified, is unfortunately mistaken. *Antipodes* was imported into English (via Latin) from the Greek *antipodes,* plural of *antipous.* As a classical import it does not have to obey the ordinary rules for English plurals. *Antipodes* is pronounced (ăn-tĭp′ə-dēz′), rhyming with *freeze.* Other English words from Greek follow a similar pattern, like *helices,* plural of *helix.*

The Greek word *antipous* literally means "with the feet opposite." In practice, the Greek word was a designation for the people living on the opposite side of the globe from an observer, so that the soles of their feet faced upward, so to speak, towards the soles of the observer.

[Middle English, people with feet opposite ours, from Latin, from Greek, from pl. of *antipous,* with the feet opposite : *anti-,* oppposite + *pous, pod-,* foot.]

asphalt (ăs′fôlt′)

noun

1. A brownish-black solid or semisolid mixture of bitumens obtained from native deposits or as a petroleum byproduct, used in paving, roofing, and waterproofing. **2.** Mixed asphalt and crushed stone gravel or sand, used for paving or roofing.

🐦 This word is properly pronounced (ăs′fôlt′), but some speakers pronounce *asphalt* as if it were a compound of existing English words and spelled "ash-fault." Using this pronunciation may imply that you are unfamiliar with the term or that you believe the bituminous substance contains ashes as a major component. Canadians, Michiganders, and Australians have claimed this variant pronunciation as a distinguishing hallmark of their speech, though there is some evidence to suggest that it occurs quite widely.

If the altered pronunciation did not arise by mistaken understanding of the composition of asphalt, it might have come about because of taboo avoidance of the word *ass*, which is a homophone of the first syllable. In any case, the sound sequence (sf) is quite common in English, appearing in words like *misfit, satisfy,* and *stressful,* as well as words of Greek origin like *asphyxiate, sphere,* and *sphinx.* So avoiding this sequence seems an unlikely motivation for altering the pronunciation.

[Middle English *aspalt,* from Medieval Latin *asphaltus,* from Greek *asphaltos.*]

In origin, **Babel** and **babble** have nothing to do with each other. **Babble** first appears in English around 1250 and is probably an example of onomatopoeia. That is, the sound of the word **babble** mimics the "ba-ba" sounds repeated by children learning to speak—and perhaps also the sounds made by the flapping lips of talkative adults.

babel also Babel (băb′əl, bā′bəl)

noun

1. A confusion of sounds or voices: *"There was a babel of talk in the air—male baritone and soprano chatter— varied by an occasional note of laughter and the swish of stiffly starched petticoats"* (Frank Norris, *The Octopus*).
2. A confusing scene or situation*: "During the 1910s and 1920s, Mexico's vernacular revolutionary culture created a babel of commemorative ceremonies, statues, and tombs sponsored by competing cults of martyred revolutionaries"* (Thomas L. Benjamin, "From the Ruins of the Ancien Régime: Mexico's Monument to the Revolution" in *Latin American Popular Culture: An Introduction*, edited by William H. Beezley and Linda A. Curcio-Nagy).

❧ The story of the Tower of Babel is told in the book of Genesis in the Bible. God notices that the people of a land called Shinar have decided to build a tower that will reach to the heavens. Concerned that human beings may overreach themselves and attempt even more grandiose projects, God resolves to do something about it (Genesis 11:6–9)*: "And the Lord said . . . 'Come, let us go down, and there confound their language, that they may not understand one another's speech.' So the Lord scattered them abroad from thence upon the face of the earth; and they left off to build the city. Therefore is the name of it called Babel; because the Lord did there confound the language of all the earth."* The Hebrew verb translated as "confound" in this passage is *balal,* which sounds a bit like *Babel.*

However, the name *Babel* does not come directly from the Hebrew verb *balal,* despite the assertion of the Biblical story. Instead, *Babel* is the Hebrew version of the name of the ancient Mesopotamian city that we call *Babylon* in English. The Babylonians themselves called their city *Babili,* which can be interpreted as meaning "gate of the god" in the Babylonian language. Modern scholars now think that the name *Babili* probably has a different origin, and that "gate of the god" is a later interpretation on the Babylonians' part. But what the name *Babili* actually meant remains unknown.

In English, the Biblical name *Babel* has traditionally been pronounced (bā′bəl), with the first syllable like the word *bay*. Older dictionaries and pronunciation manuals are unanimous on this point. Nowadays, however, some people pronounce *Babel* just like the word *babble* meaning "to speak indistinctly like a baby, prattle on" and "indistinct speech, prattling talk."

In origin, *Babel* and *babble* have nothing to do with each other. *Babble* first appears in English around 1250 and is probably an example of onomatopoeia. That is, the sound of the word *babble* mimics the "ba-ba" sounds repeated by children learning to speak—and perhaps also the sounds made by the flapping lips of talkative adults.

However, just as the ancient Hebrews tried to make sense of the name *Babel* by connecting it with their verb *balal*, "to confound," many speakers of English have also come to see a connection between the words *Babel* and *babble*. Although it is difficult to say exactly when this connection was first made, the association is a natural one. After all, the story of the Tower of Babel explains how God shattered the linguistic unity of humanity and sent people off babbling in their own tongues. In this way, the Tower of Babel was also a "Tower of Babble." The pronunciation of *Babel* as *babble* is now very common, but if you want to speak with the weight of history and tradition, say (bā′bəl). It is perhaps fitting that this word, of all words, should have a disputed pronunciation.

[After *Babel* in the Bible, a city where God confounded an attempt to build a tower into heaven by confusing the language of its builders into many mutually incomprehensible languages.]

banal (bə-năl′, bā′nəl, bə-näl′)

adjective

Drearily commonplace and often predictable; trite.

🙟 *Banal* is a word that many people avoid because it is difficult to pronounce without worry of embarrassment. This is odd because there are so many ways to pronounce it, and these pronunciations have been in use for at least a century, some much longer, and none can be considered wrong. The word can rhyme with *canal* or *anal*. Another, Frenchified pronunciation has it sounding something like *cabal*, with the stress on the last syllable, rhyming with *doll*.

Earlier in the 20th century, the British lexicographer H. W. Fowler recommended a pronunciation rhyming with *panel*, but the British have gravitated toward "buh-NAHL," with its open-wide *ah* sound. This inevitably sounds pretentious to American ears. The "BAY-nul" version is common in the US, but tends to raise eyebrows because of the echo from *anal*, and risks provoking giggles among less serious listeners. This leaves the *canal*-rhyme, which has the virtue of fitting nicely with the most common pronunciation of the related noun *banality*, whose four syllables prevent carry-over of the *panel* and *anal* rhymes. (Note that "panel-ity" is contrary to the stress pattern of English and sounds unnatural.)

Luckily, people wishing to avoid the adjective altogether have no shortage of alternatives in *commonplace, trite, pedestrian, uninspired, stale,* and many others.

[French, from Old French, shared by tenants in a feudal jurisdiction, from *ban*, summons to military service, of Germanic origin.]

boatswain (bō′sən)

noun

A warrant officer or petty officer in charge of a ship's rigging, anchors, cables, and deck crew.

🐚 Few things separate sailors from landlubbers more quickly than the pronunciation of nautical terms. At sea and on deck, the word *boatswain* is pronounced as a single word with two syllables: (bō′sən). People with sea legs have a long tradition of spelling the word as *bosun, bo's'n,* and *bos'n* to reflect the salty pronunciation. This of course has not prevented landlubbers from using the two-word pronunciation (bōt′swān′). Many other nautical words have similarly tricky shipboard pronunciations, including *bowline,* pronounced (bō′lĭn), *forecastle,* pronounced (fōk′səl) and sometimes spelled *fo'c's'le* , *gunwale,* pronounced and also sometimes spelled *gunnel, mainsail,* pronounced (mān′səl), and *topgallant,* pronounced (təgăl′ənt). With the exception of *gunwale,* however, all of these terms can be correctly pronounced as if they were two words.

[Middle English *botswein* : *bot,* boat + *swein,* mate.]

10

cache (kăsh)

noun

1. A supply of goods or store of valuables, especially when concealed in a hiding place: *We maintained a cache of food in case of emergencies.* **2.** A hiding place used especially for storing provisions or valuables.

The words *cache* and *cachet* both come from French, and they are sometimes confused. *Cache,* meaning "a store of goods stashed in a hiding place," began to appear frequently in English in the early 19th century. Thus, the police might find *a cache of drugs* hidden at a crime scene. It is properly pronounced like the word *cash.* (Note that there is no accent mark over the *e.*) *Cache* is sometimes pronounced with two syllables as (kă-shā′), but this pronunciation is not considered standard and may be viewed as a mistake by people who know French. *Cachet* means "a mark of distinction, prestige." It originally referred to a seal that closed letters and identified the writer, who was often an important person or aristocrat. Nowadays a prestigious university might attract students because it *has cachet,* or a certain brand of products might be popular because it *has a certain cachet. Cachet* is pronounced with two syllables: (kă-shā′).

[French, from *cacher*, to hide, from Old French, to press, hide, from Vulgar Latin **coācticāre,* to store, pack together, frequentative of Latin *coāctāre,* to constrain, from *coāctus,* past participle of *cōgere,* to force.]

cacophony (kə-kŏf′ə-nē)

noun

Plural: **cacophonies**

Jarring, discordant sound; dissonance.

☙ Similar as they are in spelling, the *–phony* of *cacophony* has nothing to do with being phony. The word *phony* is from *fawney,* an obsolete term for a gilded brass ring of the sort once used by swindlers to dupe unsuspecting rubes. (*Fawney* itself comes from the Irish Gaelic *faínne,* meaning simply "ring.") The root *–phony* in *cacophony,* on the other hand, comes originally from the Greek *phōnē,* meaning "sound" or "voice." The same root appears in many other words pertaining to sound, such as *euphony, symphony,* and *telephony.* Like all of these words, *cacophony* is pronounced with the stress on the third-to-last syllable and with both syllables of *–phony* unstressed: "ca-COPH-o-ny," not "CAC-o-PHO-ny."

[French *cacophonie,* from Greek *kakophōniā* , from *kakophōnos,* cacophonous : *kakos,* bad + *phōnē,* sound, voice.]

cadre (kä′drā, kä′drə, kä′dər)

noun

1. A group of trained personnel around which a larger organization can be built and trained: *a cadre of corporals who train recruits.* **2a.** A tightly knit group of zealots who are active in advancing the interests of a revolutionary party. **b.** A member of such a group.

The word *cadre* was borrowed into English from French in the 19th century. People who know some French will recognize that the word has no accent over the final *e* and so should be pronounced (kăd′rə) or (kä′dər) if the French origin of the word is to be acknowledged.

The pronunciation (kä′drā), ending in a long *a* sound, is an American invention that began as a mistake. This pronunciation probably came about by influence of the French borrowing *cachet,* whose last syllable is pronounced with an (ā) sound in both French and English. Other French borrowings like *forte,* whose last syllable is sometimes pronounced in this manner by influence of the Italian musical direction with the same spelling, are probably to blame as well. Increasing the likelihood of misinterpretation of the final *e* is the fact that many French borrowings with accented *e,* such as *protégé,* are often rendered in English writing without their accent marks.

But as often happens in language, the mistaken pronunciations of *cadre* were not recognized as such. They became widely adopted in the US. In fact, the pronunciation (kä′drā) is now the predominant one, even among the highly educated, and must be considered fully acceptable. The British, perhaps thanks to their greater exposure to the French language, are more likely to say (kä′dər).

[French, from Italian *quadro,* frame, from Latin *quadrum,* a square.]

Celtic (kĕl′tĭk, sĕl′tĭk)

adjective

Of or relating to the Celts, an Indo-European people originally of central Europe and spreading to Western Europe, the British Isles, and southeast to Galatia (in Asia Minor) during pre-Roman times.

🖋 Although many people pronounce this word with an initial (s) sound, an initial (k) sound is standard in historical, linguistic, and sociological contexts. Interestingly, the introduction of the (k) sound is a linguistic change started by scholars, contravening the historical development of the word. The *c* was probably pronounced (s), as is usual before *e*, when the word entered English from French and Latin in the 17th century. The later pronunciation with (k) imitates that of the original Latin word *Celtae*, a name for the Gauls, the ancient Celtic tribes of France. The (s) pronunciation has no doubt been reinforced by the success and popularity of Boston's professional basketball team, the Celtics, a name that is sometimes shortened to the Celts. Both are always pronounced with the (s) sound.

[From French *celtique* and Latin *Celticus* (French, from Latin), from Latin *Celtae*, the Gauls.]

Unless you are shooting the breeze with basketball fans, play it safe and pronounce the word **Celtic** as "KELL-tick." Any other pronunciation sets Irish tempers flaring.

chaise longue (shāz lông′)

noun

Plural: **chaise longues** *or* **chaises longues** (shāz lông′)

A reclining chair with a long seat that supports the outstretched legs.

🐚 Because *chaise longues* (or, if you prefer, *chaises longues*) are built for lounging, it is only natural that many English speakers should transpose the *u* and the *ng* and read *longue* as *lounge.* So many people make this mistake that *chaise longue* frequently even appears in writing as "chaise lounge." Indeed, the misspelled form may be more common than the correct form, at least in terms of its use by ordinary people. But in writing that receives the benefit of a copyeditor's scrutiny, *chaise longue* remains the preferred spelling, and "chaise lounge" is considered a mistake.

So how you should pronounce this word? The *chaise* of *chaise longue,* which would be pronounced (shĕz) in French, rhyming with our word *fez,* is generally pronounced (shāz), rhyming with *days,* in English; this pronunciation may sound odd to people with some knowledge of French, but it has the approval of most dictionaries. You should pronounce *longue* like the word *long.*

People who use the "chaise lounge" spelling despite the admonitions of all the copyeditors, dictionaries, and language sticklers often pronounce the word as "Shay's lounge" or even go further from the French original so that it sounds like "chase lounge," with an initial (ch). These pronunciations are so common that they appear as standard in some dictionaries, but they may elicit polite smiles from your more sophisticated company.

[French : *chaise*, chair (from Old French *chaire*, from Latin *cathedra*, from Greek *kathedrā* : *kata*, down + *hedrā*, seat) + *longue*, long (from Latin *longus*).]

---

chiaroscuro (kē-är′ə-skŏŏ′rō, kē-är′ə-skyŏŏ′rō)

noun

The technique of using light and shade in pictorial representation.

🐟 Hidden in the shadows of the word *chiaroscuro* are pitfalls the unsuspecting speaker of English might not see. *Chiaroscuro* comes from Italian, and the word has preserved most of the flavor of its Italian roots. It opens with a (k) sound as in *key*, not with a (ch) or (sh), as you might expect from the spelling. Many speakers approximate the Italian by pronouncing the *–scuro* part without the gliding vowel familiar to us from the related word *obscure;* that is, they say it with a simple (ŏŏ) sound, not with a (yŏŏ). The original Italian word actually has a different vowel that is long, more like our (ōō). Most dictionaries list both (ŏŏ) and (yŏŏ) as acceptable variants, but they all insist on (k) to start.

[Italian : *chiaro,* bright, light (from Latin *clārus*, clear, bright) + *oscuro,* dark (from Latin *obscūrus*).]

chicanery (shĭ-kā′nə-rē, chĭ-kā′nə-rē)

noun

Deception by trickery or sophistry.

☙ *Chicanery,* which comes from the French *chicaner* ("to trick or deceive"), offers several puzzles to English speakers. First, should the *ch–* be pronounced as an ordinary English *ch* as in *church,* or should it be pronounced softly, with a (sh) sound, as in *chevron, chic, chivalry,* and many other words whose origins are French? Generally, the (sh) pronunciation is the one preferred by educated speakers—who are, after all, the sorts of people who are most likely to employ a sophisticated word like *chicanery.*

The second puzzle concerns the *a* vowel of the second syllable. Should it be pronounced with an (ä), in the French manner, like the *a* in *façade* ("shih-connery")? Or with an (ă) as in *can* ("shih-cannery")? Or with an (ā) as in *cane* ("shih-cane-a-ree")? In this case, though most speakers retain the French *ch* sound, we have changed the vowel to suit our own tastes; the long *a* sound has become standard for the American English pronunciation of *chicanery,* just as it has for the American pronunciation of the French *charade.*

[French *chicanerie,* from *chicaner,* to use trickery or sophistry in legal proceedings, quibble, perhaps akin to French dialectal *chiquer,* to hit with a light blow.]

chimera *also* **chimaera** (kī-mîr′ə, kǐ-mîr′ə)

noun

1a. An organism, organ, or part consisting of two or more tissues of different genetic composition, produced as a result of organ transplant, grafting, or genetic engineering. **b.** A substance, such as an antibody, created from the proteins or genes of two different species. **2.** An individual who has received a transplant of genetically and immunologically different tissue. **3.** A fanciful mental illusion or fabrication: *"The passage of time is nothing real. It is a chimera spun out of gauzy consciousness, and nothing more, a frightful apparition tossed up by our mixed-up minds"* (Rebecca Goldstein, *Properties of Light*).

🐾 The word *chimera* appears primarily in scholarly and biological writing and is not often heard in speech. It comes from Greek and has an initial (k) sound like the words *chemistry* and *chorus*, as does its related adjective, *chimerical*. These words are sometimes mispronounced with (sh) at the beginning under the assumption that they come from French, like *chemise* and *chic*.

Many a graduate student has suffered painful embarrassment trying to show off a familiarity with French by pronouncing *chimera* as "SHIH-mer-a." Don't follow suit.

[Middle English *chimere*, the Chimera (a fire-breathing monster of Greek myth, usually represented as a composite of a lion, goat, and serpent), from Old French, from Latin *chimaera*, from Greek *khimaira*, she-goat, the Chimera.]

English speakers may find the pronunciation of Hebrew and Yiddish words a daunting task. In the case of **chutzpah**, however, making a rich, throaty (kh) in the right place is well worth the effort. Try it out with the next person who dares to cut in front of you on line: "The chutzpah!"

chutzpah (кʜŏ͞ot′spə, hŏ͞ot′spə)

noun

Brazen insolence; effrontery.

🙠 *Chutzpah* is a fun word to say, especially if you pronounce it as close to the original Yiddish and Hebrew as possible. *Chutzpah* begins with the sound (кʜ), a sound used in many languages of the world but not English. In German, the sound (кʜ) is found spelled *–ch* at the end of the name of the composer Johann Sebastian Bach. It is also found in the kind of English spoken in Scotland. The *Loch* in *Loch Ness* is pronounced with (кʜ).

The sound (кʜ) is actually not very difficult to make. To say (кʜ), begin by positioning your tongue far back in your mouth as if you were going to make a (k) sound. Next, instead of completely closing off the flow of air and releasing it in a distinct burst as you would for (k), you allow the air to escape through the narrow opening between your tongue and soft palate in a continuous breathy stream. If you like, you can put your tongue far enough back that the uvula (the dangling bit of flesh at the back of the soft palate) flaps against it as you breathe out; this will result in an especially rough (кʜ) sound.

In Hebrew, the (кʜ) sound is spelled with a letter called *heth.* In Yiddish, too, this letter is used to spell (кʜ) in words of Hebrew or Aramaic origin. When Hebrew and Yiddish words are written in English using the Roman alphabet, *heth* is often represented by the letter combination *ch,* as in the words *challah, Chanukah,* and *chutzpah.* When faced with the sound (кʜ) at the beginning of words of Hebrew and Yiddish origin, like *challah, Chanukah,* and *chutzpah,* many English speakers replace the (кʜ) with a simple (h) sound. Such pronunciations are listed as standard in most dictionaries, and they are reflected in alternative spellings like *hallah, Hanukah,* and *hutzpah.*

However, there is an added complication. English speakers should be aware that not every *h* in an English word of Hebrew or Yiddish origin can be pronounced as (кʜ). The Hebrew and Yiddish alphabets also have another letter, called *he,* that spells a

---

sound just like English *h* in *help*. The letter *he* is often silent at the end of Hebrew words, where it helps indicate a long "aaah" vowel at the end of a word. (The letter *h* is used in the same way in English sometimes, as in the common spellings of interjections like *Ah!* and *Oh!* The *h* in these words isn't pronounced, but rather helps indicate the length of the vowel.) The final *h*'s in *hallah, Hanukah,* and *hutzpah* are silent *he*'s, not *heth*'s. Therefore, English speakers should not attempt to pronounce these words as (κHäl′əκH), (κHä′nə-käκH), and (κHo͝ot′späκH), turning every single written *h* into a (κH). In English, *challah* is correctly pronounced as (κHäl′ə) or (häl′ə), *Hanukah* as (κHä′nə-kə) or (hä′nə-kə), and *hutzpah* as (κHo͝ot′spə) or (ho͝ot′spə).

Because of the problems that arise when we try to write Hebrew or Yiddish words in the Roman alphabet, English speakers may find the pronunciation of words from Hebrew and Yiddish a daunting task—unless you know these languages, it may be difficult to know whether an *h* represents a (κH) or a silent Hebrew *h*. In the case of *chutzpah*, however, making a rich, throaty (κH) in the right place is well worth the effort. Try it out with the next person who dares to cut in front of you on line: "The chutzpah!"

[Yiddish *khutspe,* from Mishnaic Hebrew *ḥuṣpâ,* from *ḥāṣap,* to be insolent.]

19

claddagh (klä′də)

noun

A ring with a raised design of two hands clasping a crowned heart, usually given as a token of love or friendship.

🐚 Words that have been borrowed from the Irish language and preserved their original Irish spelling in some measure can present special challenges to those unfamiliar with Ireland or Irish. For instance, the name of the town south of Dublin traditionally spelled *Dún Laoghaire* is often spelled *Dunleary* in English and pronounced (dŭn-lē′rē). Most Irish place names have an Anglicized version of the name that is much more reader-friendly to an English speaker. *Shillelagh*, the word for the bulbous-headed wooden club made from blackthorn wood, is pronounced (shə-lā′lē). It is named after the village of Shillelagh (or *Síol Éalaigh* in Irish) in County Wicklow, where there is a forest that has traditionally provided the wood for the clubs.

Claddagh is another word that comes from an Irish place name. It is pronounced (klä′də), the best approximation that Americans can make of the sound of the word as pronounced in English and as spoken in Ireland. The *gh* is silent in *claddagh*. The claddagh ring gets its name from Claddagh, once a simple fishing village on the shores of Galway Bay on the west coast of Ireland but now part of the city of Galway. *Claddagh* is the English form of the village's name in the Irish language, *an Cladach,* which literally means "the flat, stony seashore." Claddagh rings have long been popular in parts of the west coast of Ireland, including Connemara, the Aran Islands, and the shores of Galway Bay, but they became especially associated with the village of Claddagh. The earliest known examples of claddagh rings were made by a goldsmith working in Galway around three hundred years ago.

There are various traditional ways of wearing the rings to indicate the wearer's romantic availability or the degree to which the wearer has accepted the love of the person who has given the ring. According to one system, when the ring is worn on the right hand with the heart pointing to the fingertip, the wearer's heart is still available to anyone, so to speak. When worn on the right hand with the heart pointing to the wrist, the wearer has a sweetheart, but no promises have been made yet. When worn on the left hand with the heart pointing to the fingertip, the wearer is engaged. And when worn on the left hand with the heart pointing to wrist, prospective suitors are out of luck—the wearer is married. However, other conventions of interpretation exist, and some people ignore them altogether when they put on their rings, so a claddagh is not always an infallible indicator of the wearer's romantic life.

[After *Claddagh*, a fishing village and suburb of Galway.]

coccyx (kŏk′sĭks)

noun

> Plural: **coccyges** (kŏk-sī′jēz, kŏk′sĭ-jēz′)

A small triangular bone at the base of the spinal column in humans and tailless apes, consisting of several fused rudimentary vertebrae. Also called *tailbone.*

❧ If *coccyx* presents a pronunciation challenge to you, you can probably blame that problem on two factors that lie not in you but in the word itself. The first factor is its rarity. Ubiquitous as the coccyx certainly is, the word *coccyx* is uncommon outside of hospitals, anatomy classes, and other medical contexts. For those of us who are not doctors and have no wish to be, *tailbone* means much the same thing and is clearer. The second factor is its opacity. *Coccyx* simply isn't made up of the familiar roots, prefixes, and suffixes that so often help us to guess the probable pronunciation of unfamiliar words like *convolve, transduction,* or *antidisestablishmentarianism.*

However, there is a useful phonetic rule to help you make sense of *coccyx.* The *cc* consonant pair is pronounced as a (k) sound when it comes immediately before *a, o, u,* or a consonant, as in *staccato, accommodate, accuse,* and *acclimate.* It is pronounced (ks) when it precedes *e* (as in *accent*), *i* (as in *vaccine*), or *y.* Thus *coccyx* is pronounced (kŏk′sĭks), with a (ks) sound. The only significant exception to this *cc* rule has to do with words borrowed from Italian. In these words, such as *bocce, capriccioso,* and *fettuccine,* the *cc* preceding an *e* or *i* is pronounced with an ordinary English (ch).

[New Latin, from Greek *kokkūx,* cuckoo, coccyx (from its resemblance to a cuckoo's beak).]

coitus (koit′əs, kō′ĭ-təs, kō-ē′təs)

noun

Sexual union between a male and a female.

🖎 This scientific-sounding word is more likely to be seen than heard, and so it is not surprising that its pronunciation is quite variable. The oldest pronunciation, (kō′ĭ-təs), has three syllables, with the stress on the first, and sounds a little like "go at us." A second pronunciation, (kō-ē′təs), places stress on the second syllable, which has the vowel of *see,* sounding somewhat like "delete us." A third, (koit′əs), has only two syllables, the first of which is identical in sound to our word *coy.* It is probably the most common pronunciation among Americans nowadays.

All three pronunciations are in widespread use by educated speakers, many of whom consider the other two (whichever they might be) to be incorrect. Another variant, having the vowel of *eye* in the second syllable, and sounding a bit like the disease *colitis,* is less common and may provoke guffaws.

So you may pronounce *coitus* in any of three ways and rightfully consider yourself to be correct. Just don't expect many other people to agree with you.

[Latin, from past participle of *coīre,* to copulate : *co-,* with + *īre,* to go, come.]

comptroller (kən-trō′lər, kŏmp-trō′lər, kŏmp′trō′lər)

noun

An officer who audits accounts and supervises the finances of a corporation or governmental body.

🙠 Etymologically speaking, a comptroller is simply someone who controls, or checks and verifies, accounts. The word descends from a Latin word *contrārotulātor* that literally means "counter-roller, a person who checks accounts against a duplicate register." Our verb *control* comes from the related Latin verb *contrārotulāre,* "to check by duplicate register." So a comptroller is simply a special kind of controller.

When the word *comptroller* appeared in English in the early 1400s, it had various spellings without a *p,* such as *countrollour.* But a variant spelling with a *p* soon arose through association of the first part of the word, *cont–,* with the etymologically unrelated word *count,* which in medieval times was also spelled *compte.* English *count* (or *compte*) derives from the Old French *conter* (or *compter*), which in turn comes from Latin *computāre,* "to compute."

Historically, *comptroller* was pronounced just like *controller,* and remains so today. But as more people learned to read and saw the letters *–mp–,* the spelling pronunciations (kŏmp-trō′lər) and (kŏmp′trō′lər) became widespread. They have long been included in dictionaries and must be considered acceptable, even if they don't slip so easily off the tongue.

[From a variant spelling (influenced by *counten, compten,* to count, from Old French *conter, compter,* from Latin *computāre,* to sum up, compute) of Middle English *countrollour,* accountant, from Anglo-Norman *countreroullour,* from Medieval Latin *contrārotulātor,* from *contrārotulāre,* to check by duplicate register, from *contrārotulus,* duplicate register : Latin *contrā-,* against + Latin *rotulus,* roll, diminutive of *rota,* wheel.]

---

conch (kŏngk, kŏnch)

noun

    Plural: **conchs** (kŏngks) *or* **conches** (kŏn′chĭz)

1. Any of various tropical marine gastropod mollusks, especially of the genera Strombus and Cassis, having large, often brightly colored spiral shells and edible flesh. **2.** The shell of one of these gastropod mollusks, used as an ornament, in making cameos, or as a horn.

🐚 Among those who are familiar with *conchs* as seafood, the *ch* in the name of these mollusks is usually pronounced (k). The word ultimately comes from Greek *konkhē,* "mussel," by way of Latin *concha.* The letters *ch* had the hard sound of (k) in Latin, by the way, never a soft pronunciation like English (ch). In Middle English, the word *conch* was sometimes spelled *conk* or *congh*, which indicates that the pronunciation with (k) has long been in use.

    However, some people nowadays say (kŏnch), with a final (ch). This is perhaps a spelling pronunciation initiated by people who were unfamiliar with the spoken word. It is also possible that the pronunciation with (ch) reflects a borrowing of the word from French, not directly from Latin. In medieval times, as Latin developed into Old French in France, Latin *concha* became Old French *conche.* The Old French word was pronounced roughly (kōɴch) and generally meant "a shell," or "a shell-shaped receptacle." *Conche,* now pronounced (kōɴsh), survives today in Modern French with the meaning "a basin or enclosed body of water in a salt marsh." The Modern English pronunciation (kŏnch) may reflect the separate borrowing of the French word or its influence.

    In any case, both pronunciations of *conch,* (kŏngk) and (kŏnch), are widespread and acceptable. However, if you want to pronounce the word as people do who live where the ocean is warm enough for conchs to be caught and eaten fresh, use the pronunciation that rhymes with *bonk*.

[Middle English *conche,* from Old French, from Latin *concha*, mussel, from Greek *konkhē.*]

concupiscence (kŏn-kyo͞o′pĭ-səns)

noun

A strong desire, especially sexual desire; lust.

۞ *Concupiscence,* meaning "a strong sexual desire, lust," is not a word you are likely to hear at a nightclub or cocktail party. The word has a long history of use by Christian theologians, coming from Latin *concupiscentia,* who often contrasted it with *caritas,* the source of our word *charity.* Traditionally, *concupiscence* is pronounced with the primary stress on the second syllable (kŏn-kyo͞o′pĭ-səns). An alternative pronunciation with primary stress on the third syllable (kŏn′kyo͞o-pĭs′əns) is a more recent and less standard innovation. If you want to sound like you've read some theology, use the traditional pronunciation.

[Middle English, from Old French, from Late Latin *con-cupīscentia,* from Latin *concupīscēns, concupīscent-,* present participle of *concupīscere,* to conceive a strong desire for, from *concupere,* to desire strongly : *com-,* intensive prefix + *cupere,* to desire.]

coup de grâce (ko͞o′ də gräs′)

noun

Plural: **coups de grâce** (ko͞o′ də gräs′)

1. A deathblow delivered to end the misery of a mortally wounded victim. **2.** A finishing stroke or decisive event.

🖙 The French phrase *coup de grâce,* "stroke of mercy," was originally used to describe a deathblow delivered to end the misery of a mortally wounded victim. From there it was extended to indicate any finishing stroke or decisive event. Miswriting and mispronouncing the phrase *coup de grâce* as "coup de gras" (ko͞o′ də grä′)—literally, "stroke of fat"—will certainly put a decisive end to a reader's confidence in the author of a piece of writing. This common error among English speakers probably results from the influence of other well-known phrases of French origin found in English, such as *Mardi Gras* and the name of the delicacy *foie gras,* "fattened goose liver." In English, these are usually pronounced (mär′dē grä′) and (fwä grä′), respectively, as approximations of their original French pronunciations. The error "coup de gras" may also reflect a mispronunciation based on the widespread knowledge that many letters found in the written form of French words are silent in pronunciation, in particular, final *s*. Among English speakers otherwise unfamiliar with the French language, the pronunciation of the (s) sound at the end of French *grâce* may then come to be perceived as an error, although it is in fact correct.

   Coup de grâce is pronounced (ko͞o′ də gräs′) in English. The French noun *grâce,* "grace, favor, a kindness" found in this phrase is the source of English *grace* and is related to the well-known Spanish expression *gracias,* "thanks." These facts may help English speakers remember the correct pronunciation.

[French : *coup,* blow + *de,* of + *grâce,* grace, favor.]

Pronounce this word "coo duh grahss," not "coo duh grah"—that would mean "stroke of fat" in French. A French person might think you were talking about slapping something with a piece of bacon.

covert (kō′vərt, kō-vûrt′, kŭv′ərt)

adjective

Not openly practiced, avowed, engaged in, accumulated, or shown: *covert military operations; covert funding for the rebels.*

🐚 This word, which is related to *cover,* is traditionally pronounced (kŭv′ərt), with the same stress as the word *cupboard.* The vowel *o* is given the same pronunciation as it is in the related verb *cover.* In fact, *covert* simply means "covered" in Old French.

In the 20th century, American English developed a variant pronunciation with a long *o* in the first syllable, (kō′vərt), and over the past forty years or so this pronunciation has become predominant. You hear of spy agencies running covert operations with a long *o,* almost never with a short *u.* The pronunciation with a short *u* remains common in British English, however. The development of the long *o* may have come about by influence of the antonym *overt,* which is pronounced with a long *o.* While both pronunciations must be considered acceptable, using the traditional pronunciation will probably wrinkle some brows on the foreheads around you. Use the one with the long *o.* Both *covert* and *overt* can be acceptably pronounced with stress on the first or second syllable, though *overt* is not frequently given stress on the second syllable like *avert.* *Covert* tends to have its stress on the first syllable when it succeeds a noun, as in *covert operations,* but the stress often falls on the second syllable when the adjective is freestanding, as in *The operation was classified as covert.*

[Middle English, from Old French *covert,* from past participle of *covrir,* to cover, from Latin *cooperīre,* to cover completely : *co-,* intensive prefix + *operīre,* to cover.]

cumin   (kŭm′ĭn, kōō′mĭn, kyōō′mĭn)

noun

1. An annual Mediterranean herb (*Cuminum cyminum*) in the parsley family, having finely divided leaves and clusters of small white or pink flowers. **2.** The seedlike fruit of this plant used for seasoning, as in curry and chili powders.

🌿 The word *cumin* has a long history in English, dating back to the 9th century or earlier, but it wasn't always spelled as it is now. Earlier spellings, in roughly chronological order, include *kymen, cymen, comyn, commen, cummin,* and *commin*. These forms reflect the fact that, historically, the word *cumin* has a short vowel in its first syllable, not a long one. In fact, for several centuries, culinary authorities and lexicographers have favored the pronunciation (kŭm′ĭn), sounding very much like "come in" but with stress on the first syllable. But recently, this pronunciation has been losing ground to pronunciations that sound like "coomin" (kōō′mĭn) and "cue-min" (kyōō′mĭn). At this point, both these pronunciations are more widely used by educated speakers than the traditional pronunciation is.

[Middle English, from Old French, from Latin *cumīnum,* from Greek *kumīnon,* probably of Semitic origin and akin to Arabic *kammūn* and Hebrew *kammōn*.]

daiquiri (dăk′ə-rē, dī′kə-rē)

noun

Plural: **daiquiris**

An iced cocktail of rum, lime or lemon juice, and sugar.

🐦 The name of the village of Daiquirí in Cuba is pronounced (dī-kē-rē′), as if the first syllable were the English *die*. The cocktail that takes its name from that village, however, has undergone a pronunciation change in the mouths of most English speakers. The original (ī) pronunciation of *ai* is not exactly a single vowel but a diphthong—a speech sound produced by starting with one vowel sound and quickly blending it into another. To produce an (ī) sound, for instance, you start with an *ah* sound (ä) and quickly slide into an *ee* sound (ē). Many English speakers replace the diphthong (ī) with a much simpler (ă), making *daiquiri* sound like "dackery." Although there are still some people who will quibble that this newer pronunciation is wrong, it is nevertheless the most common pronunciation of the word in the US today. The older, more historically correct pronunciation is also widely accepted but may sound odd, especially to younger listeners.

[After *Daiquirí,* a village of eastern Cuba.]

debacle (dĭ-bä**′**kəl, dĭ-băk**′**əl, dĕb**′**ə-kəl)

noun

1. A sudden, disastrous collapse, downfall, or defeat; a rout. **2.** A total, often ludicrous failure. **3.** The breaking up of ice in a river. **4.** A violent flood.

This word was borrowed from French as *débâcle* some two hundred years ago, but it has since shed its accent marks. Originally *debacle* referred to the breaking up of ice in a river, what we now often call *ice-out*, preferring as English speakers often do, a compound of familiar and time-honored English words to an unfamiliar word that is hard to say without making some oral adjustments. The original *debacle* also referred to the huge flood of water that roars down a river after ice-out.

These senses still exist in English but are rare in comparison to the metaphorical meaning of a disastrous failure or collapse. For instance, *debacle* is often applied to financial disasters like the savings and loan crisis of the late 1980s and the dot-com implosion on Wall Street that rang in the new millennium. But the word is hardly limited to finance and can refer to any sort of disaster that results from human folly.

The pronunciation of the word presents a challenge, since like most French borrowings, the word has undergone some distortions in becoming Anglicized, and this process is ongoing. Many people continue to pronounce this word with a broad *a* in the second syllable (to rhyme with the *Bock* of *Bock beer*), as (dĭ-bä**′**kəl), or less commonly as (dā-bä**′**kəl), reflecting the French spelling with an accent over the first *e*. Note that the stress is on the second syllable. The pronunciation with the second syllable sounding like the word *back*, (dĭ-băk**′**əl), has long been established as standard. The pronunciation (dĕb**′**ə-kəl), with stress on the first syllable, is becoming more common and may supplant the others in time because it fits the stress pattern of other English words like *miracle* and *spectacle*.

This is a case in which you really can't go wrong—or right—since the pronunciation of the word is in flux, and some people may flinch no matter how you say it. Luckily, there are many handy substitutes, like *disaster, collapse, failure,* and *mess,* and there is no shortage of modifiers like *colossal* and *gigantic* to help out, if you want to avoid the matter.

[French *débâcle,* from *débâcler,* to unbar, from Old French *desbacler* : *des-,* in the opposite or reverse way + *bacler,* to bar (from Vulgar Latin **bacculāre,* from Latin *baculum,* rod).]

30

desuetude (dĕs′wĭ-to͞od′, dĕs′wĭ-tyo͞od′)

noun

A state of disuse or inactivity: *"As it happens I have never heard an author say that he did use dictation; this seems to be a method of the Erle Stanley Gardner generation that has fallen into desuetude"* (Stephen Fry, "Forget Ideas, Mr. Author. What Kind of Pen Do You Use?" *New York Times*).

✍ The word *desuetude* is itself largely in desuetude—that is, it has fallen into a state of disuse. Outside of the legal profession, where *desuetude* is not in desuetude at all, but enjoys a continuing usefulness, you are unlikely to hear the word spoken and likely to read it only in self-consciously erudite works. Many readers and speakers, therefore, have no idea how it should be pronounced. Obviously the *–tude* is pronounced "tood," as in *attitude, fortitude,* or *solitude*. But the rest of the word presents a challenge. Based on the pronunciation of the word *suet* (which is, of course, completely unrelated except in its spelling), many people assume that *desuetude* should be pronounced as a four-syllable word, with primary stress on the second syllable, much along the lines of *decrepitude* and *definitude*. However, the traditional pronunciation combines the *ue* into a single syllable and places the primary stress on the first syllable, as "DESS-wi-tood."

[French *désuétude,* from Latin *dēsuētūdō,* from *dēsuētus,* past participle of *dēsuēscere,* to put out of use : *dē-,* from, out of + *suēscere,* to become accustomed.]

desultory (děs′əl-tôr′ē, děz′əl-tôr′ē)

adjective

1. Having no set plan; haphazard or random: *"then
some desultory reading, starting with the newspaper and
a couple of* National Geographics *I'd picked up at a yard
sale"* (T. Coraghessan Boyle, "Tooth and Claw," *The
New Yorker*). **2.** Moving or jumping from one thing to
another; disconnected: *"She had suddenly begun speaking, after sitting silently through several hours of desultory discussion with her husband about the Resistance"*
(Adam Nossiter, *The Algeria Hotel*).

෴ Most of the common four-syllable *–tory* words in English follow the same rhythmic pattern, being stressed on their first and
third syllables, as in the familiar *dormitory, inventory, lavatory,
mandatory,* and *predatory.* But there are a number of less common words, like *olfactory, perfunctory,* and *refectory,* that are
stressed on the second syllable only. *Desultory,* which belongs to
a distinctly literary register of English—you rarely hear it in everyday conversation—may seem as if it belongs in this second
group, but it actually is pronounced in the more common way,
with stress on its first and third syllables.

[Latin *dēsultōrius,* leaping, from *dēsultor,* a leaper, from
dēsultus, past participle of *dēsilīre,* to leap down : *dē-,* from,
out of + *salīre,* to jump.]

detritus (dĭ-trī′təs)

noun
   Plural: **detritus**

1. Loose fragments or grains that have been worn away from rock. **2.** Accumulated or waste material: *"We walked through a flea market . . . one stall after another filled with monogrammed coffee spoons, amateur watercolors, faded table linens folded in pale tissue, the detritus of comfortable bourgeois lives"* (Joan Didion, "History Lesson," *Travel and Leisure*).

✍ The word *detritus* is sometimes mispronounced as (dĕ′trĭ-təs), as if it were accented on the first syllable and rhymed with the medical words *fremitus, habitus,* and *vomitus*. All four of these words are derived from Latin, but there is an important difference between *detritus* and the other three. In Latin, *fremitus, habitus,* and *vomitus* have a short *i* and are stressed on the first syllable. The Latin word *detrītus* has a long *i,* which was pronounced in Roman times with a sound roughly like English *ee* (ē). In Latin, the stress in *detrītus* was on the long *i*. In English borrowings from Latin, the Latin long *i* often came to be pronounced like English *eye*. These facts are reflected in (dĭ-trī′təs), the correct English pronunciation of English *detritus,* rhyming with *fight us*.

[French *détritus,* from Latin *dētrītus,* from past participle of *dēterere,* to lessen, wear away.]

Diaspora (dī-ăs′pər-ə)

noun

1. The dispersion of Jews outside of Israel from the sixth century BC, when they were exiled to Babylonia, until the present time. **2.** often **diaspora** The body of Jews or Jewish communities outside Palestine or modern Israel. **3.** **diaspora a.** A dispersion of a people from their original homeland. **b.** The community formed by such a people.

℘ᴂ The pronunciation of *diaspora* is almost impossible to deduce from the spelling. Is it pronounced with stress on the first and third syllables, like *diabetes, diagnosis,* and *dialectic*? Or with stress on the second syllable, as in *diaconate, dialysis,* and *diaphanous*? *Cyclospora*, the only other *–spora* word in the *American Heritage Dictionary*, is pronounced (sĭk′lə-spōr′ə), stressing the first and third syllables—in the *diabetes* manner. But tradition dictates that *diaspora* be pronounced (dī-ăs′pər-ə), with the stress on the second syllable as in *dialysis*; the "di-a-SPO-ra" pronunciation, with stress on the third syllable, is widely considered an error, much like the "ple-THO-ra" pronunciation of *plethora*.

For some reason, many people who put the stress on the correct syllable use a long *e*, as in *deep*, instead of a long *i*, as in *cry*, in the first syllable. But few dictionaries condone this pronunciation, and given that nearly all the other *dia–* words use the long *i*, your best bet is to use the long *i* in *diaspora* as well.

[Greek *diasporā*, dispersion, from *diaspeirein*, to spread about : *dia-*, through, throughout + *speirein*, to sow, scatter.]

(34)

divisive (dǐ-vī′sǐv)

adjective

Creating dissension or discord: *divisive topics such as tax policy.*

🖎 Probably influenced by the closely related word *division*, many people pronounce the second vowel of *divisive* with a short *i* as in *pit*. But *divisive* is traditionally pronounced (dǐ-vī′sǐv), with the stressed syllable having a long *i* as in *pie*. Properly pronounced, *divisive* thus rhymes with *decisive*. The pronunciation with a short *i* in the second syllable, rhyming with *dismissive*, is considered by many people to be a mistake.

[From Latin *dīvīsus,* past participle of *dīvidere,* to divide + English *-ive,* adjectival suffix (from Middle English, from Old French, from Latin *-īvus*).]

dour (do͝or, dour)

adjective

    Comparative: **dourer**
    Superlative: **dourest**

Marked by sternness, harshness, or ill humor; forbidding or gloomy: *"The families, though distantly related, had feuds that went back hundreds of years and by now had hardened into a dour sullenness"* (Edna O'Brien, *Wild Decembers*).

🖎 This word, which is etymologically related to *duress* and *endure*, traditionally rhymes with *tour*. But a variant pronunciation (probably a spelling pronunciation) that rhymes with *sour* has been in use for a century or more and is widely used today. It is listed as a standard variant in most dictionaries.

    In contrast to so many other words listed in this book, *dour* has not seen its traditional pronunciation fade away, and it still has great currency. In fact, many people consider it the only correct way to pronounce the word.

[Middle English, possibly from Middle Irish *dúr,* probably from Latin *dūrus,* hard.]

elegiac (ĕl′əl-jī′ək, ĭ-lē′jē-ăk′)

adjective

Of, relating to, or involving elegy or mourning or expressing sorrow for that which is irrecoverably past: *"While making a commercial recording of the book, White himself choked as he read those elegiac words about Charlotte—'and no one was with her when she died'— so that the taping session had to be stopped"* (Peter F. Neumeyer, "E. B. White," in *The Essential Guide to Children's Books and Their Creators,* edited by Anita Silvey).

☙ *Elegiac* is frequently not only mispronounced but misspelled— it has a long history of appearing in print as "elegaic." Most likely this confusion has to do with the fact that the suffixes *–iac* (as in *aphrodisiac, cardiac,* and *hypochondriac*) and *–aic* (as in *archaic, formulaic,* or *photovoltaic*) are both used in English to designate adjectives. Furthermore, these endings are about equally common. Adding to the difficulty is the fact that *elegiac* is a term borrowed from classical literature, a field that has given us such *–aic* words as *prosaic, spondaic,* and *trochaic.* Educated English speakers, aware that an elegy is a classical poem of lament, are thus especially likely to be misled into mispronouncing *elegiac* as if it were spelled "elegaic." If you wish to pronounce it in a way that reflects the actual *ia* spelling, your best bet is to pronounce it (ĕl′ə-jī′ək), with the stress on the third syllable as in *paranoiac.* The pronunciation (ĭ-lē′jē-ăk′), with the stress on the second syllable as in *insomniac,* is also accepted by many dictionaries but is much less common.

[Late Latin *elegīacus,* from Greek *elegeiakos,* from *elegeia,* elegy, plural of *elegeion,* unit of verse in which elegies were composed, from *elegos,* song, mournful song.]

epitome (ĭ-pĭt′ə-mē)

noun

1. A representative or perfect example of a class or type: "*Legs was more impressed by Norman's friend Harold Conrad, who regaled the punks with stories about promoting fights in the 1940s and drinking at the Copacabana, and seemed the epitome of cool*" (Mary V. Dearborn, *Mailer*). **2.** A brief summary, as of a book or article; an abstract: *Chapter one serves as an epitome of the work as a whole.*

☞ The word *epitome* is properly pronounced with four syllables, with the stress on the second (*pit*). Its last two syllables rhyme with the last two in *anatomy*. People sometimes mispronounce the word with three syllables, as if the last syllable rhymed with *home*.

[Latin *epitomē*, a summary, from Greek, an abridgment, from *epitemnein*, to cut short : *epi-*, on, upon + *temnein*, to cut.]

It is simply incorrect to pronounce **epitome** as if the last part of the word was the big book called a tome. In fact, the older meaning of **epitome** is more like the opposite of a tome, as it refers to a brief summary of something. Properly spoken, **epitome** has four syllables like **anatomy**.

epoch (ĕp'ək, ē'pŏk')

noun

1. A particular period of history, especially one considered remarkable or noteworthy. **2.** A unit of geologic time that is a division of a period.

🖘 When vowels are unstressed, they tend to become somewhat less distinct in their pronunciations. For example, the *e* of *manner* and the *o* of *manor* are so similar in their sound that in ordinary speech they sound almost exactly the same. The same might be said of the first *e* in *cowered* and the *a* in *coward*.

The vowel sounds in the second syllables of *epic* and *epoch* (as *epoch* is most commonly pronounced) are not precisely the same; *epic* is pronounced with a short *i,* and *epoch* with a schwa (ə). But the two pronunciations are close enough to cause confusion, particularly when dealing with sentences such as *Charlemagne is the central figure of the medieval epoch* and *Charlemagne is the central figure of the medieval epic.* One sentence refers to Charlemagne's position in history, the other to his role in the heroic poem *La Chanson de Roland.* This is perhaps why some speakers use the pronunciation (ē'pŏk'), like "EE-pock." This may not be the approved pronunciation in the United States, but it does have the virtue of eliminating all possibility of confusion between *epoch* and *epic.*

[Medieval Latin *epocha,* measure of time, from Greek *epokhē,* a point in time.]

err (ûr, ĕr)

intransitive verb
> Past participle and past tense: **erred**
> Present participle: **erring**
> Third person singular present tense: **errs**

1. To make an error or a mistake. **2.** To violate accepted moral standards.

🐾 Most people today do not pronounce *err* to rhyme with *fur*, but this pronunciation, (ûr), is the older, traditional, and historically correct one. The pronunciation (ĕr), in which *err* sounds like *air*, has gained widespread currency, perhaps as a result of association with *errant* and *error,* which derive from the same Latin verb meaning "to wander."

You are also correct if you pronounce the word to rhyme with *fur.* You may be seen as trying to preserve a relic, however.

[Middle English *erren,* from Old French *errer,* from Latin *errāre,* to wander.]

feng shui (fŭng′ shwā′)

noun

The Chinese art or practice of positioning objects, especially graves, buildings, and furniture, based on a belief in patterns of yin and yang and the flow of chi that have positive and negative effects.

Feng shui is a traditional Chinese practice that seeks to improve people's quality of life by encouraging the beneficial flow of chi, the vital force believed in Taoism and other schools of Chinese to be inherent in all things. The unimpeded circulation of chi, and a balance of its negative and positive forms in the body, are held to be essential to good health. Practitioners of feng shui try to improve the flow of chi by creating propitious arrangements of the physical world based on the opposition of yin (the passive, female cosmic principle in traditional Chinese philosophy) with yang (the active, male cosmic principle). The Chinese term for this practice, *fēng shuǐ,* makes reference to a passage in an early manual of feng shui in which the wind (*fēng)* is said to carry chi until it is stopped by water (*shuǐ*).

Even though the word is spelled *feng shui,* the usual Anglicized pronunciation of the word sounds as if it were spelled "fung shway" (fŭng shwā) or "fung shwee" (fŭng shwē). In fact, the pronunciation "fung shway" (fŭng shwā) is a pretty good approximation of the way the word sounds in Mandarin Chinese.

Chinese is often referred to as a single language with many dialects, such as Mandarin, Cantonese, Shanghainese, and Taiwanese. However, the differences between these different "dialects" are as great as the differences between English and German or between French and Spanish, which we think of as being different languages. Historically, the Mandarin "dialect" of Chinese, spoken over a large area including much of the north of China, has been used for official business throughout China. Today, the official language is based on the kind of Mandarin spoken in the capital Beijing.

Chinese is usually written in Chinese characters, of course, but the Chinese government has adopted an official system for spelling Mandarin words in the Roman alphabet when this is necessary. This system goes by the name of *pinyin* in English, from the Mandarin term *pīnyīn* (made up of *pīn,* "to connect," and *yīn,* "sound.") The sound values of some letters in pinyin are quite different from the values of the same letters in English. For example, the letter *q* is pronounced approximately like English (ch), as in *qīng,* "clean, pure," pronounced roughly (ching). The four different tones of Mandarin are indicated by diacritical marks placed above the vowels. For example, *dā,* pronounced with the voice at a high pitch that stays the same throughout the word, means "to put up, build," while *dá,* pronounced with the voice starting at a medium pitch and rising to a high pitch, means "to answer." The word *dǎ,* with a pitch that falls and then rises, means "to hit," while the word *dà,* with a pitch that starts out high and falls low, means "big." In pinyin, the vowel *e* often has a sound like English (ŭ) or (ə), and the letter sequence *ui* is pronounced like English *way* (wā). The English spelling of *feng shui,* pronounced (fŭng shwā), is simply the pinyin spelling of the Mandarin term *fēng shuǐ* with the tone marks removed.

[Chinese (Mandarin) *fēng shuǐ,* wind (and) water : *fēng,* wind + *shuǐ,* water.]

flaccid (flăs′ĭd, flăk′sĭd)

adjective

1. Lacking firmness, resilience, or muscle tone. **2.** Lacking vigor or energy: *flaccid management.*

🙝 Entering English by alteration of Latin *flaccidus* as far back as the 1600s, our word *flaccid* should have had its pronunciation settled by now. And for a long time, it did. The older pronunciation is (flăk′sĭd), having a (k) sound from the Latin source, and following the (ks) pattern of most words in English with the letters *–cc–* in the middle, words like *accept, accident, eccentric,* and *vaccinate.* All of these words come from Latin, by the way.

Since the natural tendency of language users is to regularize usage into easy-to-use patterns, you would think that English speakers would have been content to leave well enough alone: *Flaccid* fits neatly with the other *–cc–* words. But the variant pronunciation without a (k) sound, (flăs′ĭd), arose sometime in the first half of the 20th century and has become increasingly common, to the point where most educated speakers pronounce the word with the (s) sound, to rhyme with *acid* and *placid.*

Why this change should have occurred is something of a mystery. Perhaps people feel that a soft (s) sound in the middle of *flaccid* is more appropriate for a word meaning "lacking firmness, soft, flabby." Perhaps the rhyme with *placid* has considerable gravitational pull. But these days the (s) pronunciation is more common even among educated speakers than the (ks) pronunciation.

[Latin *flaccidus,* from *flaccus,* flabby.]

forbade (fər-băd′, fər-bād′, fôr-băd′, fôr-bād′)

verb

A past tense of *forbid.*

🐾 Like *bid* itself, *forbid* is what linguists call a strong verb, a verb that has a vowel in its past tense (*forbade*) and past participle (*forbidden*) that is different from the vowel of its base form or present tense (*forbid*). English has many verbs like this, such as *ride* (*rode, ridden*), *swim* (*swam, swum*), and *give* (*gave, given*).

Over the centuries, many strong verbs have seen their past tense forms change as speakers have tried to simplify and regularize the complex English verb system. Since the 1400s, *forbid* had a past tense spelled *forbad.* This was sometimes also spelled *forbade.* The traditional pronunciation of *forbad* and *forbade* has been (fər-băd′), sounding like "for bad." But by a reinterpretation of the spelling *–bade*, people at some point began to pronounce *forbade* as a rhyme of *grade.*

Recently, a more "regular" past tense, *forbid,* has arisen. This form is sometimes used as a past participle as well (as it is in the verb *bid*), giving us a single form for the base form, past tense, and past participle after the model of verbs like *burst, cut,* and *split.* The past tense *forbade* is still standard, but is starting to have an archaic feel. Pronouncing it to rhyme with *had* puts the weight of history on your side, though in this case that may not be such a good thing. The pronunciation that rhymes with *blade* is unjustified by the word's lengthy history but has been used widely enough to be listed in most dictionaries for several decades. You can also use *forbid* as a standard past tense, keeping in mind that the only standard past participle—so far—is *forbidden.*

But check back in ten years. The situation is likely to have changed.

[Middle English *forbad, forbade,* from earlier Middle English *forbed, forbead* (influenced by *bad,* past tense of *bidden,* to request), from Old English *forbēad,* past tense of *forbēodan,* to forbid.]

forte (fôr-tā′, fôrt)

noun

1. Something in which a person excels: *"He wanted to know about those surprises ahead of time. His forte was in defusing negative rumors before they ever exploded into news accounts that could reach the public"* (Jane Mayer and Jill Abramson, *Strange Justice*). **2.** The strong part of a sword blade, between the middle and the hilt.

☙ This word, meaning "strong point," comes from French *fort,* a monosyllable also meaning "strong point," though originally the strong point was literal—the hilt end of a sword blade. So our word *forte* is pronounced quite correctly like our word *fort.*

But as with *flaccid* and *err* and countless other words, something got in the way of this neat picture. The something in this case was the Italian musical direction *forte,* meaning "loud." The Italians pronounce their final *e*'s, so the Italian word has two syllables, with the *e* pronounced roughly like our letter *a.* English speakers familiar with music thought that *forte,* "strong point," (from French *fort*) was the same two-syllable word as Italian *forte,* and this pronunciation, (fôr-tā′), has probably become the more common of the two. The two-syllable pronunciation was an American invention of the 20th century.

A second complicating factor, one that reinforced the two-syllable pronunciation, was the tendency of accent marks to be disused in English. Words like cliche, protege, and naivete all had accent marks originally, but like most diacritics in English these marks seemed more trouble than they were worth and often were ignored. If the final *e* in *cliche* is pronounced, why not the final *e* in *forte*?

People who want to adhere more closely to the etymology of the word should use the one-syllable pronunciation. Correcting users of the two-syllable version might seem pedantic, however. Speak and let speak.

[French *fort,* from Old French, strong, from Latin *fortis.*]

geisha (gā′shə, gē′shə)

noun
Plural: **geishas** or **geisha**

One of a class of professional women in Japan trained from girlhood in conversation, dancing, and singing in order to entertain professional or social gatherings of men.

✤ The word *geisha* is often pronounced (gē′shə). This pronunciation has a long history in popular American culture. For instance, (gē′shə) is the pronunciation used by country music star Hank Locklin in his song "Geisha Girl" from 1957. Although the pronunciation (gē′shə) has been common in American speech for a long time, nowadays (gē′shə) may smack a little of the days of the Allied occupation of Japan after World War II, and to some people, it may suggest a patronizing attitude toward Asian cultures.

The pronunciation (gā′shə), however, is much closer to the original pronunciation of the word in Japanese. The Japanese word *geisha* is made up of the elements *gei,* "art, skill," and *sha,* "person." A geisha undergoes rigorous training to acquire a variety of skills to make professional and social gatherings enjoyable and relaxing. She learns to dress her hair and apply make-up in the elaborate style that distinguishes her profession. She learns to sing traditional songs, dance traditional dances, and play traditional instruments like the shamisen to entertain her guests. And she must become witty and clever at conversation to help smooth things over when moments of social awkwardness arise, or her guests begin to dispute.

In the world outside Japan, there has been a great deal of misunderstanding about the role of the geisha at Japanese social gatherings and the nature of her relationship with her patrons—the geisha offers her clients nothing more than the grace of her speech and performances and the beauty of her face and attire, to be admired at a respectful distance. Nowadays, people who pronounce *geisha* as (gē′shə) may—however unwittingly—give the impression that they are ignorant about Japanese culture and perhaps even insensitive to the role of the geisha.

[Japanese : *gei*, art (from Middle Chinese *ŋejh*, equivalent to modern Mandarin *yì*) + *sha*, person (from Middle Chinese *tšiaʔ*, equivalent to modern Mandarin *zhě*).]

genre (zhän′rə)

noun

A category of artistic composition, as in music or literature, marked by a distinctive style, form, or content.

🌿 In French, the *n* of the word *genre* is not pronounced as the consonant (n) sound. Instead, the *n* shows that the vowel preceding it is what linguists call a *nasal vowel*. In pronouncing an ordinary vowel, you produce sound by allowing air to escape through your mouth. Nasal vowels are pronounced similarly, except that in making a nasal vowel you lower your soft palate so that air resonates in your nasal passages and passes out your nose as well as your mouth. Both French and English have nasal vowels, but in English, this nasalizing happens automatically (and unconsciously) before the consonant sounds (m), (n), and (ng); it does not serve to distinguish one word from another, and it is not indicated by the pronunciation symbols in most English dictionaries. In French, however, the simple difference between a nasal vowel and an ordinary vowel can make a huge difference. For example, the feminine form of the French word for "tired" is spelled *lasse* and pronounced (läs). The word for "lance" is spelled *lance* and pronounced with a nasalized version of the vowel sound (ä) but no consonant (n) sound.

The French word *genre* poses particular difficulties for English speakers—it has a nasal vowel before *r*, which is rolled in the back of the throat in French, and this combination is completely unlike anything in English. Many English speakers, therefore, pronounce *genre* as (zhän′rə), with an ordinary English (ä) sound (as in *father*) and an ordinary English (n) sound. This pronunciation is widespread enough among educated speakers to be generally acceptable. It is somewhat less acceptable to pronounce *genre* as (jän′rə), as if the first syllable were *John*.

[French, from Old French, kind, from Latin *genus, gener-*.]

gnocchi (nyō′kē, nyŏk′ē)

plural noun

Dumplings made of flour, semolina, or potatoes, boiled or baked and served with grated cheese or a sauce.

🏵 There's no good reason why *gnocchi* ought to be difficult for English speakers to pronounce. Admittedly, the spelling is confusing because of the differences between the ways Italian and English represent spoken sounds in writing. Particularly troublesome is the *gn–*, which English speakers are tempted to pronounce with a simple (n) sound when it comes at the beginning of a word (as in *gnarled, gnome,* or *Gnostic*), and the *–ch–*, which one might easily assume is pronounced in *gnocchi* as it is in familiar English words like *church, inch,* or *parch*. The *gn–* is pronounced like the letters *–ny–* in the middle of *canyon* or like the letters *gn–* in the thoroughly Americanized word *lasagna*. The *–cchi* is simply pronounced like the English word *key*.

[Italian, plural of *gnocco,* probably alteration of *nocchio,* knot in wood.]

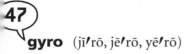

gyro (jī′rō, jē′rō, yē′rō)

noun

Plural: **gyros**

A sandwich made usually of sliced roasted lamb, onion, and tomato on pita bread.

🍃 Standing in line to order a *gyro* at a Greek restaurant, you may hear the word *gyro* pronounced (jī′rō) or (yē′rō), or sometimes you may even hear the sandwich called a (yē′rōs). What should you say when you order?

The word *gyro* comes from Modern Greek, rather than Ancient Greek like most other English words of Greek origin. The Modern Greek word for a gyro, when transliterated into the Roman alphabet, is *gyros.* To the ears of a speaker of English, this Modern Greek word sounds something like (yē′rōs). In actuality, the letter *g* in this transliteration does not have a (y) sound, but something between a (y) and a (zh) sound. Linguists call this sound a *voiced palatal fricative,* and (y) is the best approximation a speaker of English can make to it.

For the singular form of the word for the Greek-style sandwich, many Americans say *gyros,* pronounced (yē′rōs), rather than *gyro* without an *s.* For example, they might say, "I had a great gyros at that joint on the corner," rather than "I had a great gyro." In Greek, *gyros* is actually the form that the word takes when it is singular and used as the subject of the sentence. When the word functions as the direct object (or as the object of most prepositions), it takes the form *gyro,* without an *s.* Some Americans of Greek descent may insist upon the singular subject form *gyros* in English, while others are content with using *gyro* as the singular form in English—pronounced like (yē′rō), of course. It has also been suggested that the English spelling *gyro* results from a misinterpretation of the Greek singular *gyros* as a plural. English speakers, when they first encountered the word *gyros* in written form, may have thought that the word was plural, since it ended in -*s*. They then removed the -*s* to create a new English singular *gyro*. The same process has occurred in another word of Greek origin, *kudos*.

In Greek, the word *gyros* literally means "a turn, an act of turning." The word makes reference to the turning of the meat near the flame as it revolves around the vertical spit on which it is skewered. Modern Greek *gyros* is directly descended from the Ancient Greek word *gyros*, which also means "a turn." Ancient Greek *gyros* is the ultimate source of all of the other English words that refer to turning and contain the element *gyr*– or *gyro*–, like *gyre, gyrate,* and *gyroscope.* The *gyr*– in these words is pronounced (jīr). This is because the Greek word-building element *gyro*– was borrowed into Latin when the Greek letter gamma (transliterated *g*) still had a (g) sound, rather than with the *y*-like sound of a voiced palatal fricative. Beginning several centuries ago, English in turn began to borrow the Latin words that contained the *gyr*– and *gyro*– *prefix* from Greek *gyros.* When English borrowed these words, the *g* before the vowels *i, y,* and *e* was pronounced (j), as in *gyrate* (jī-rāt′).

Later, when the Greek style of roasting and serving meat was introduced into North America by immigrants, the Modern Greek word *gyros* began to be written down on English-language menus and the like. The spelling of *gyro* must have encouraged some English speakers to pronounce the word as (jī′rō), like all the other words of Greek origin that began *gyro*-. Greek Americans who heard Greek being spoken at home, and other Americans familiar with the Modern Greek pronunciation, kept the original sound of the word, (yē′rōs) or (yē′rō).

[From Modern Greek *gyros,* a turning, from Greek *gūros,* circle (from the turning of the meat on a spit).]

Standing in line to order a **gyro** at a Greek restaurant, you may hear the word **gyro** pronounced "JIE-roh" or "YEE-roh," or sometimes you may even hear the sandwich called a "YEE-rohs." What should you say when you order?

Halley's comet (hăl'ēz, hā'lēz)

noun

A comet with a period of approximately 76 years. The first comet for which a return was successfully predicted, it last appeared in 1986.

🌠 Halley's comet is named for the 17th-century English astronomer Edmund Halley, who analyzed astronomical data from the past and successfully predicted the reappearance of the comet in 1758. Ideally, we should base our pronunciation of the comet's name on the correct pronunciation of the astronomer's. Unfortunately, it is far from certain how Halley pronounced his own name; most British people of the name *Halley* today pronounce their name as if it rhymed with *valley,* but some historical authorities argue that the correct 17th-century pronunciation would be (hô'lē) as if the spelling were "Hawley." In fact, the spelling of the astronomer's name as "Hawley" is well attested in writings of that period.

There is also the perennially popular (hā'lē) (as in "Hey, Lee!"), which is probably not historically correct but has been reinforced in the public imagination by the name of the 1950s rock-'n'-roll band Bill Haley and His Comets. This pronunciation, though common, is less widely accepted than the pronunciation rhyming with *valley.* Your best bet, probably, is to go with the latter option—bearing in mind, however, that even that form might sound wrong to Halley himself, if he were to return from the grave and hear people discussing the next expected arrival of his comet in AD 2061.

[After Edmund *Halley* (1646–1742), English astronomer.]

harass (hə-răs′, hăr′əs)

transitive verb

    Past participle and past tense: **harassed**

    Present participle: **harassing**

    Third person singular present tense: **harasses**

1. To subject (someone) to hostile or prejudicial remarks or actions; pressure or intimidate. **2.** To irritate or torment persistently: *He was harassed by doubts and misgivings.* **3.** To make repeated attacks or raids on (an enemy).

The pronunciation with stress on the first syllable is the older, traditional pronunciation, when the word was adopted into English in the 1600s. The pronunciation with stress on the second syllable is a newer pronunciation, dating from the 19th century. It is yet another American variation in pronunciation that was initially and for decades afterwards denounced as an ignorant mistake. Nonetheless, its use has steadily increased since the middle of the 20th century, and it is now the predominant pronunciation in the US. It appears to be growing in British English as well.

The motivation for this change is hard to determine. The pronunciation that rhymes roughly with *terrace* has nothing troublesome about it and is not an aberration in English stress patterns. Moreover, there is no preexisting pattern of similar-sounding words with stress on the second syllable to tempt speakers away from the traditional pronunciation. The only real rhymes in English are *surpass* and the archaic *alas*.

Certainly there are words that rightly or wrongly shift stress from the first to the second syllable, such as *despicable* and *desuetude*, but these words have more than two syllables. A sizable number of two-syllable words (along with some three-syllable words), most of them deriving from French or Latin, shift stress from the first to second syllable when the part of speech changes from noun to verb: words like *address, contract, discount, permit,* and *record* (note that you break a *record*, but *record* an interview). It is possible that *harass* developed its newer pronunciation to accord with this pattern, even though it has no noun.

But no one can be sure about this, so the mystery of *harass* and *harassment* abides. If you want to ride the wave of the future, put the stress on the second syllable, and bid tradition goodbye.

[French *harasser,* possibly from Old French *harer,* to set a dog on, from *hare, haro,* interjection used to set a dog on, of Germanic origin and akin to English *here.*]

50

hegemony (hǐ-jěm′ə-nē, hěj′ə-mō′nē)

noun

Plural: **hegemonies**

The predominant influence, as of a state, region, or group, over another or others.

Only the dustiest of pedants prefer the hard *g* sound in *hegemony.* This pronunciation is rooted in the word's Greek etymology, but English is well-supplied with words in which the Greek gamma is pronounced as a *j*—*genealogy* and *geometry,* for example. Some dictionaries list the hard-*g hegemony* as an option, but by far the most accepted pronunciation—the one listed first by dictionaries and actually used by the vast majority of speakers—is the one in which the *g* is pronounced with a (j) sound.

As for the placement of the speech stress or accent, it is interesting to note that unlike most other *–mony* words (*alimony, ceremony, testimony,* etc.), *hegemony* is usually pronounced with stress on the second syllable, not the first and third.

[Greek *hēgemoniā,* from *hēgemōn,* leader, from *hēgesthai,* to lead.]

hovel (hŭv′əl, hŏv′əl)

noun

1. A small, miserable dwelling. **2.** An open, low shed.

In American English *hovel* is most commonly pronounced with a short *u* sound in the first syllable, as (hŭv′əl), rhyming with *shovel*. Less commonly, it is pronounced with a short *o*, as (hŏv′əl), rhyming with *novel*. The opposite is true of the apparent rhyme *grovel*, where short *o* (grŏv′əl) predominates over short *u* (grŭv′əl). This discrepancy is not easy to sort out because the etymology of *hovel* remains unclear. Judging by the pronunciations given in dictionaries, the one with short *u* appears to be fairly recent, perhaps a 20th-century innovation. To vote with the majority, you would *grovel*—with (ŏ)—in a *hovel*—with (ŭ).

[Middle English, hut.]

52

impious (ĭm′pē-əs, ĭm-pī′əs)

adjective

Lacking reverence; not pious.

  ☜ The traditional pronunciation is (ĭm′pē-əs), with stress on the first syllable, and a long *e* as in *me* in the second. The pronunciation (ĭm-pī′əs), with stress on the second syllable and a long *i* as in *pie* instead of a long *e*, stands as another mistake that in modernity became too popular to be considered wrong. The "pious" pronunciation has been included in dictionaries since the middle of the 20th century and is now the most common pronunciation.

[From Latin *impius : in-,* not + *pius,* dutiful.]

53

jejune (jə-jo͞on′)

adjective

1. Not interesting; dull: *"Next to these superb appetizers, clams posillipo, baked clams and cold antipasto seemed jejune"* (M. H. Reed, "Three Star Dining in Granite Springs," *New York Times*). **2.** Lacking maturity; childish: *"[his] jejune credulity as to the absolute validity of his ideals and the unworthiness of the world in disregarding them"* (George Bernard Shaw, *Arms and the Man*).

  ☜ English speakers who have learned a smattering of French are probably responsible for the current state of the word *jejune*. Originally meaning "famished" or "devoid of useful content," it later acquired a secondary sense of "immature or childish," probably because people assumed the *–june* was cognate with the French *jeune,* "young." (It is actually related to the French *déjeuner,* which originally meant "a breaking of a fast.") Mistaken as that connection is, the newer meaning of *jejune* is now firmly enough established in English that few educated speakers would consider it wrong. However, the direct ancestor of *jejune* is not French but the Latin *iēiūnus*, so there is little rationale for the pronunciation that replaces the English (j) sound with a Frenchified (zh), as (zhə-zhōōn′).

Such erroneous Frenchified pronunciations of *j* as (zh) are commonly introduced in English words whose foreign origins are apparent to speakers of English. Some people seem to feel that the (zh) sound is more appropriate in exotic words than a plain old English (j), despite that fact that (zh) is found in such everyday English words as *division* and *vision*. For example, the name of the capital of China is pronounced as if it were *Beizhing*, when actually *Beijing* with (j) is a much better approximation of the Chinese pronunciation. Similarly, in the Hindi and Sanskrit originals of English words like *Raj* and *maharaja*, the *j* is pronounced just like English (j). There is no need to substitute a (zh) sound for this *j*, though many people do nonetheless.

[From Latin *iēiūnus*, meager, dry, fasting.]

kiln (kĭln, kĭl)

noun

Any of various ovens for hardening, burning, or drying substances such as grain, meal, or clay, especially a brick-lined oven used to bake or fire ceramics.

☙ *Kiln* is another word in which what was lost has been restored. Deriving from Latin *culina*, "oven" (also the source of our word *culinary*), *kiln* originally had a final (n) sound. It was spelled *cyln* in Old English, for example. But the (n) was lost in a reduction of a consonant cluster, in the same way that the final (n) was lost from the word *mill* (which was in Middle English *mulne* or *mylne*, a borrowing of Late Latin *molina*).

The (n) in *kiln* began its disappearance in the 1400s, but was restored several centuries later as a spelling pronunciation. The word was sometimes spelled with an *n* and sometimes without. People who could read often saw the *n* in the spelling, and naturally thought it should be pronounced. This practice caught on, and now there are two acceptable ways of saying the word. Nonetheless, the pronunciation with (n) has largely displaced the one that rhymes with *hill*.

[Middle English *kilne*, from Old English *cyln*, from Latin *culīna*, kitchen, stove.]

kudos (ko͞o′dōz′, ko͞o′dōs′, ko͞o′dŏs′, kyo͞o′dōz′, kyo͞o′dōs′, kyo͞o′dŏs′)

noun

Acclaim or praise for exceptional achievement.

🖎 *Kudos* is one of those words that looks plural but is etymologically singular. It takes its place beside certain other words of Greek origin like *topos* (whose plural is properly *topoi*) and *pathos.* Acknowledging this history requires you to say *Kudos is* [not *are*] *due her for her brilliant work.* But because it looks like an English plural, *kudos* has often been treated like one, as in *She received many kudos for her work.* This plural use has given rise to the singular form *kudo,* as in *The award added yet another kudo to her prize-laden career,* but this usage, and the plural usage evident in *many kudos,* are widely considered to be errors.

These developments follow the pattern of the English words *pea* and *cherry. Pea* started out centuries ago as *pease,* still heard in the rhyme beginning *Pease porridge hot, pease porridge cold.* (The plural of *pease* was usually *peasen,* like *ox* and *oxen.*) At some point, *pease* was interpreted as a plural, and the *s* was dropped to make a new singular *pea.* The word *cherry* has a similar history. It comes from *cherise,* the word for "cherry" in the Norman dialect of Old French (the corresponding word in modern French is *cerise*). English speakers apparently took French *cherise* as a plural and made a new singular *cherry.* No one is complaining about these blunders today—they have become standard—but the status of *kudos* is still up in the air.

Interestingly, many people who are careful to treat *kudos* as a singular noun tend to pronounce it as if it were a plural. Students of Greek know that the final consonant in words like *kudos* and *pathos* is pronounced as an (s), rhyming with *loss.* More often than not, however, *kudos* is pronounced in English with a (z) to rhyme with *doze.* Insisting on the Greek pronunciation will probably be seen as pedantic, however. Both pronunciations are acceptable, but it seems safest to rhyme the word with *rose.*

[Greek *kūdos,* magical glory.]

lingerie (län′zhə-rā′, län′zhə-rē, lăn-zhə-rē′)

noun

1. Women's underwear. **2.** *Archaic* Linen articles, especially garments.

🙠 The most widely accepted pronunciation of *lingerie* has a pleasingly French feel to it. Most of us pronounce its first syllable *lin–* with the vowel (ä) as in the name *Don*, which recalls the sound of French *la*, "the"; its second syllable has the (zh) of the English *rouge*, from the French word *rouge*, "red"; and the *–rie* is pronounced like the *–ré* of *émigré* or the *–rée* of *soirée*. Unfortunately, this pronunciation bears little relation to the actual French pronunciation of *lingerie*; if we want to be more accurate we should give *lin–* the vowel (ă) sound as in *pat* and *–rie* the sound of *ee* as in *free*. But of course pronunciation is not a matter of absolute authenticity but of broad consensus, and it appears that the faux-French pronunciation of *lingerie* has achieved such a consensus among American speakers of English. *C'est la vie.*

[French, from Old French, from *linge,* linen, from Latin *līneus,* made of linen, from *līnum,* flax.]

Of course pronunciation is not a matter of absolute authenticity but of broad consensus, and it appears that the faux-French pronunciation of **lingerie** (as "lahn-zhe-RAY") has achieved such a consensus among American speakers of English. *C'est la vie.*

loath (lōth, lō*th*)

adjective

Unwilling or reluctant; disinclined: *I am loath to go on such short notice.*

The combination of letters *th* is usually pronounced one of two ways in English: unvoiced as in *think* or voiced as in *then.* Both sounds are produced by letting air escape through a narrow space between tongue and teeth; the primary difference between them is that in the *th* of *think* the vocal cords do not vibrate, whereas in the *th* of *then* they do. These two sounds are, obviously, quite similar, and in some English words like *with,* the *th* can be pronounced either voiced or unvoiced as you prefer. But in other cases a difference of pronunciation results in a different meaning or part of speech; for instance, the *th* of *cloth* is always unvoiced, while the *th* in *clothe* is always voiced. The reason for this is purely historical; there was a time when *th* was voiced when it fell in the middle of a word and unvoiced at the end of a word, so in the Middle English verb *clothen* ("to put clothes on") the *th* was voiced, while the *th* in the noun *cloth* ("fabric or material") was unvoiced. The modern English *loathe* and *loath* are from the Middle English *lathen* and *lath,* respectively, so they too follow this historic rule.

[Middle English *loth,* displeasing, loath, from Old English *lāth,* hateful, loathsome.]

long-lived (lông′līvd′, lông′lĭvd′)

adjective

1. Having a long life: *a long-lived aunt.* **2.** Lasting a long time: *a long-lived rumor.*

🐾 How you pronounce this word, and its counterpart *short-lived,* depends on how you mentally break them down into their constituent parts. Most people probably think of this word as coming from the verb *to live,* when in fact the word was formed in Middle English times as a compound of *long* and the noun *life,* plus the suffix *-ed.* This is the same suffix that we see in other compound adjectives, like *sad-eyed* and *long-haired.*

The change from *-lifed* to *-lived* occurred because the suffix *–ed* was always pronounced as a full syllable in Middle English, so *long-lifed* had three syllables. The *f* was voiced between the two vowels as (v), by the same rule that gave us the plural form *lives* from the singular noun *life.* Eventually people began to spell the word *long-lived* to reflect the pronunciation.

And sometime after that, people began to pronounce the word as it was spelled, as (lông′lĭvd′), as if it came from the verb *live* instead of the noun *life.* The "lived" pronunciation was denounced in various usage guides for much of the 20th century, but it multiplied nonetheless and has been included in dictionaries as standard since the early 1990s.

The happy result of this involved history is that you can pronounce the word either way and know you can't be wrong. The mistakes are buried safely in the past.

[Middle English *long-lifed* : *long,* long + *life,* life + *-ed,* having.]

machination

(măk′ə-nā′shən, măsh′ə-nā′shən)

noun

A crafty scheme or cunning design for the accomplishment of a sinister end.

🖎 *Machination* was borrowed into English in the 1400s from both French and Latin, and the French and Latin words ultimately come from Greek. The traditional pronunciation of this word is (măk′ə-nā′shən), with the *ch* pronounced (k), as it is in other English words derived from Greek like *archetype, bronchus,* and *echo.* The pronunciation (măsh′ə-nā′shən), with the *ch* pronounced (sh), is a relatively new variant and has been given alongside the other pronunciation in most dictionaries since about the middle of the 20th century.

Perhaps one reason for the change is the association of *machination* with its etymological cousin *machine,* which derives from the same Greek ancestor but came into English in the 1500s through the intermediary of French. The (k) pronunciation, however, remains more common and more widely accepted than the (sh) pronunciation. You can't go wrong with (k).

[From Old French *machination* and Latin *māchinātiō, māchinātiōn-* (French, from Latin), from Latin *māchinārī, māchināt-,* to design, contrive, plot, from *māchina,* device, from Greek *mākhanā,* dialectal variant of *mēkhanē.*]

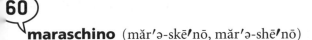

60

maraschino (măr′ə-skē′nō, măr′ə-shē′nō)

noun

Plural: **maraschinos**

A cordial made from the fermented juice and crushed pits of the marasca cherry.

ℱ Generally, *–sch–* is pronounced (sh) when the word it occurs in was borrowed from German or Yiddish (as in *borscht, mensch, schist,* or *schnauzer*), and it is pronounced (sk) when the word it occurs in was borrowed or derived from Italian, Latin, or Greek (as in *bruschetta, scheme, scherzo,* or *school*). Since *maraschino* is from Italian, its proper pronunciation follows the latter pattern, having the (sk) sound rather than (sh). The (sh) pronunciation is widely used and accepted by many dictionaries, but if you have any aspiration to be recognized as a gourmet, you should probably stick with the (sk).

[Italian, from *marasca,* marasca, the variety of cherry used to make the cordial, from *amarasca,* from *amaro,* bitter, from Latin *amārus.*]

marquis (mär′kwĭs, mär-kē′)

noun

Plural: **marquises** (mär′kwĭ-sĭz)
or **marquis** (mär-kēz′)

A nobleman ranking below a duke and above an earl or a count.

The most familiar marquis, to most Americans, is probably Comte Donatien Alphonse François de Sade, the "Marquis de Sade" from whose name we derive the nouns *sadist* and *sadism.* You may also remember the Marquis de Lafayette, one of the heroes of the American Revolution. Both were French; we are therefore most familiar with the French pronunciation of *marquis,* (mär-kē′), with stress on the second syllable and with a silent *s.*

But the title of *marquis* exists in Great Britain as well, where it is traditionally pronounced (mär′kwĭs), with stress on the first syllable and with the *s* fully pronounced. In British contexts, the spelling *marquis* has largely been supplanted by the variant *marquess* as well. A Scottish *marquis,* however, is still very often a *marquis,* pronounced (mär′kwĭs), rather than a *marquess.* The only British marquess likely to be familiar to Americans is the Eighth Marquess of Queensberry, who in the 19th century promoted a code of rules for the sport of boxing.

Your best guideline for pronouncing *marquis,* then, is to use the French pronunciation (mär-kē′) when referring to French noblemen and the British pronunciation (mär′kwĭs) when referring to British noblemen. To make matters more complicated, the feminine title corresponding to the French *marquis* is *marquise,* pronounced (mär-kēz′), while the feminine title corresponding to the British *marquess* is *marchioness,* pronounced (mär′shə-nĕs) or (mär-shə-nĕs′).

[French *marquis* and Middle English *marques,* both from Old French *marchis,* marquis, from *marche,* border country, of Germanic origin.]

metastasize (mĭ-tăs′tə-sīz′)

intransitive verb

Past participle and past tense: **metastasized**
Present participle: **metastasizing**
Third person singular present tense: **metastasizes**

1. To be transmitted or transferred by metastasis.
2. To be changed or transformed, especially danger-ously: *"a need for love that would metastasize into an in-satiable craving for attention"* (Michiko Kakutani, *New York Times Book Review*). **3.** To spread, especially de-structively: *"[disinformation] . . . that even now contin-ues to metastasize . . . to such a degree that myth threat-ens to overthrow history"* (Gore Vidal, *The New Yorker*).

🍳 The prefix *meta–* is normally pronounced with stress on its first syllable; so is the word *stasis*, to which the *–stasize* of *metastasize* is closely related. But the verb *metastasize* is pronounced with stress not on its first but on its second syllable, and so is the noun *metastasis*—but not the adjective *metastatic*.

In addition to stressing the correct syllable (the *–tas–* of *metastasize*, the *–stat–* of *metastatic*), you should of course make sure you get all the consonants correct. Don't say "metastathize" or "metasthetize," as if the word were constructed along the lines of *sympathize* or *anesthetize*. Such a pronunciation, which may come about because speakers find it difficult to remember or coordinate the four alternating (t) and (s) consonant sounds in the word, is simply incorrect.

[From *metastasis* (from Greek, shifting place, departure, change, from *methistanai,* to place in another way, change : *meta-,* later, beyond + *histanai,* to cause to stand, place) + *-ize,* verb suffix.]

mischievous (mĭs′chə-vəs)

adjective

1. Causing or tending to cause mischief: *a mischievous child.* **2.** Causing harm, injury, or damage: *mischievous rumors and falsehoods.*

❧ The four-syllable pronunciation (mĭs-chē′vē-əs) occurs with some frequency but is generally considered nonstandard and does not appear in most dictionaries. However, the four-syllable version of this word has been in use for some five hundred years and cannot be considered an upstart. There are many words that end in the same way, and these probably exert some ongoing gravitational pull—words like *abstemious, delirious, hilarious,* and *imperious.* It would seem then that this is one variant pronunciation whose time has come. Nonetheless, the spelling ending in *–ious* is routinely called out by authorities like English professors and copyeditors as a mistake, and so the corresponding pronunciation remains tainted.

    Mischievous is traditionally and properly pronounced (mĭs′chə-vəs), with three syllables and the stress on the first syllable.

[Middle English *mischevous,* from *mischef,* mischief, from Old French *meschief,* misfortune, from *meschever,* to end badly : *mes-,* badly + *chever,* to happen, come to an end (from Vulgar Latin **capāre,* to come to a head, from Latin *caput,* head).]

moot (mo͞ot)

adjective

1. Subject to debate; arguable: *"It is a moot point whether Napoleon Bonaparte [who was born in Corsica] was born a subject of the King of France"* (Norman Davies, *Europe: A History*). **2.** Of no practical importance; irrelevant: *"[He] was appearing as a goodwill gesture, since the competition was moot for him; he had long ago qualified for inclusion in the games"* (Mark Levine, "The Birdman," *The New Yorker*). **3.** Not presenting an open legal question, as a result of the occurrence of some event definitively resolving the issue, or the absence of a genuine case or controversy.

❧ Many mispronunciations arise from a reader's inability to guess the proper pronunciation of a word he or she has seen in print but has never heard. Others come about through a different mechanism: the attempt to make sense of a word one has heard spoken but never seen in print. This sort of error often manifests itself in the replacement of the unfamiliar word with a more familiar one that is similar in sound and at least superficially related in meaning. Such is the case with *moot*. Since a moot question is one whose interest is purely academic or not worth serious discussion—a question that does not speak to us with much urgency—some speakers of English assume that *moot* is the same as *mute*, and they pronounce it as such, with a (yo͞o) instead of a simple (o͞o) vowel. But this is a mistake, and it glosses over the significant difference in meaning between the two words. Someone who is *mute* is silent; something that is *moot* is debatable but not of immediate importance.

[From such Early Modern English compounds as *moot-book,* book of hypothetical cases to be argued by law students, from Middle English *moot,* meeting, argument, law case, from Old English *mōt, gemōt,* meeting, assembly, akin to Old English *mētan,* to meet.]

mores (môr′āz′, môr′ēz′)

plural noun

The accepted traditional customs and usages of a particular social group.

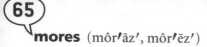 This word, which comes from Latin and means "customs" or "ways," has two syllables and may be pronounced with either a long *a* or a long *e* sound in the second syllable. The pronunciation with a long *a* sound, which is probably the more common one in contemporary English, is closer to a Classical Latin pronunciation, while the pronunciation with a long *e* is an Anglicized Latin pronunciation.

Pronouncing the word with one syllable will make you sound like a Neanderthal.

[Latin *mōrēs,* plural of *mōs,* custom.]

Neanderthal (nē-ăn′dər-thôl′, nē-ăn′dər-tôl′,
nā-än′dər-täl′)

noun

1. a. An extinct human species (*Homo neanderthalen-sis*) or subspecies (*Homo sapiens neanderthalensis*) living during the late Pleistocene Epoch throughout most of Europe and parts of Asia and northern Africa. **b.** An individual belonging to this species or subspecies. **2.** *Slang* A crude, boorish, or slow-witted person.

☙ The modern German language does not make use of the (th) sound, either voiced (as in the English *then*) or unvoiced (as in the English *thin*). Historically, German did use *th* in spelling many words, but this *th* represented a (t) sound. The word *Neanderthal* comes from the name of a valley in Germany where the remains of prehistoric humans were discovered in 1856. Long after the discovery of the prehistoric remains and long after the adoption of the German *Neanderthal* into English as a name for the people whose remains they were, 20th-century spelling reforms in Germany changed the written *th* in words like *Thal* ("valley") to a simple *t*, so that the standard German name for *Homo neanderthalensis* is now *Neandertaler,* not *Neanderthaler.* But the English name, unaffected by the German reform, usually retains the 19th-century *th* spelling. Regardless of how it is spelled, in scientific and scholarly contexts, *Neanderthal* should be pronounced with the (t) sound. As used by laypeople, especially in colloquial and metaphorical contexts, it is quite often pronounced with a (th) sound, and this pronunciation is widely accepted by dictionaries.

[After *Neanderthal* (Neandertal), a valley of western Germany near Düsseldorf.]

niche (nĭch, nēsh)

noun

1. A recess in a wall, as for holding a statue or urn. **2.** A cranny, hollow, or crevice, as in rock. **3. a.** A situation or activity specially suited to a person's interests, abilities, or nature: *She finally found her niche in life.* **b.** A special area of demand for a product or service: *books published for a niche.* **4.** *Ecology* **a.** The function or position of an organism or population within an ecological community. **b.** The particular area within a habitat occupied by an organism.

※ Since *niche* was borrowed from French in the 17th century, and Anglicized shortly thereafter, you might think that its pronunciation would be both settled and unremarkable. But think again. Many French borrowings (like those mentioned in this book) have troublesome pronunciations because most English speakers can't speak French very well, if at all. *Niche* presents a counterexample to this pattern: it was quickly converted into a comfortable English-sounding word, pronounced (nĭch) and rhyming with *itch.* But in the 20th century, people familiar with French thought that a word that looked French should sound French, and so the francophone pronunciation (nēsh), rhyming with *quiche,* was revived.

Although some Americans consider this pronunciation to be an affectation (note that it is standard in Britain), it is included in most American dictionaries. The hybrid pronunciation (nēch), which takes something from each version to rhyme with *leech,* is even less favored, perhaps because it makes you look as though you don't know what language you're speaking.

[French, from Old French, from *nichier,* to nest (from Vulgar Latin **nīdicāre,* from Latin *nīdus,* nest) or from Old Italian *nicchio,* seashell (perhaps from Latin *mītulus,* mussel).]

nuclear (nōō′klē-ər, nyōō′klē-ər)

adjective

1. *Biology* Of, relating to, or forming a nucleus of a cell: *a nuclear membrane.* **2.** *Physics* Of or relating to atomic nuclei: *a nuclear chain reaction.* **3.** Using or derived from the energy of atomic nuclei: *nuclear power.* **4.** Of, using, or possessing atomic or hydrogen bombs: *nuclear war; nuclear nations.*

🖉 Few pronunciations have come under such scathing condemnation and comic scorn as the "nucular" pronunciation of *nuclear,* which is now frequently viewed as a telltale sign of ignorance, stupidity, or worse.

Users of this pronunciation might protest. After all, the pronunciation (nōō′kyə-lər) presents a prime example of how a familiar phonological pattern can influence an unfamiliar one. The usual pronunciation of the final two syllables of this word is (-klē-ər), but this sequence of sounds is rare in English (it exists in *pricklier,* for instance). Much more common is the similar sequence (-kyə-lər), which occurs in words like *particular, circular, spectacular,* and in many scientific words like *molecular, ocular,* and *vascular.* It is interesting to note that in Roman times the word *nucleus* had two different competing pronunciations, just as the English word *nuclear* does today. Some ancient Romans pronounced and spelled the word *nucleus* as "nuculeus," with a *u* between the *c* and the *l,* similar to the *u* that pops up in the modern American pronunciation "nucular."

Adjusted to fit into this familiar pattern, the (-kyə-lər) pronunciation is often heard in high places. It is not uncommon in the military, even among commanders, in association with nuclear weaponry, and it has been observed in the speech of US presidents, not all of them verbal blunderers like Dwight D. Eisenhower (who was famous for his incoherent off-the-cuff remarks in press conferences) and George W. Bush. The highly literate Jimmy Carter and the polished extemporaneous speaker Bill Clinton are also given to using this pronunciation. Most of these people are southerners or from the southern half of the United States, suggesting that the pronunciation might have originated as a regional one.

The prominence of many of these speakers, however, has done little to brighten the appeal of (nōō′kyə-lər), and many educated speakers consider it unacceptable. Use it at your peril.

[From *nucleus* (from Latin *nuculeus, nucleus*, kernel, from *nucula*, little nut, diminutive of *nux, nuc-*, nut) + *-ar*, adjective suffix.]

oblique (ō-blēk**'**, ə-blēk**'**)

adjective

1. Having a slanting or sloping direction, course, or position; inclined. **2.** *Mathematics* Designating geometric lines or planes that are neither parallel nor perpendicular.

There is a historic pronunciation of *oblique* in military contexts that uses a long *i* as in *pie* in the second syllable, making *oblique* rhyme with *alike*. This martial tradition notwithstanding, in all other contexts it is most proper to pronounce the word with a long *e* as in *me*, rhyming with *unique*. Whatever you do, don't pronounce it as if the *–que* were a separate syllable like the *–qué* of *risqué*.

[Middle English, from Old French, from Latin *oblīquus.*]

oeuvre (œ′vrə)

noun
   Plural: **oeuvres** (œ′vrə)

1. A work of art. **2.** The sum of the lifework of an artist, writer, or composer.

🐝 *Oeuvre* is rarely used in everyday English speech, possibly because its meaning tends to limit its usefulness to contexts having to do with the fine arts. The related word *hors d'oeuvre,* on the other hand, has attained a wide currency in American speech, because everybody has to eat. As a result, the pronunciation of *hors d'oeuvre* has been radically modified to a form (ôr-dûrv′) that trips easily off the Anglophone tongue. Meanwhile, *oeuvre* has remained relatively unmodified. You must not pronounce it simply (ûrv), rhyming with *nerve,* or (o͞o′vər), rhyming with *Hoover,* or (o͞o′vrə). You must purse your lips and attempt to reproduce the sound of the French vowel (œ), tacking on the *–vre* very lightly, almost as an afterthought. Although the vowel (œ) is not found in native English words, it is a very common sound in many other languages such as French and German. To make (œ), say the vowel (ĕ) as in *let* while rounding your lips in the same way as you do when you say the vowel (ō) as in *low.*

[French *œuvre,* from Old French *uevre,* work, from Latin *opera,* from plural of *opus,* work.]

often (ô′fən, ôf′tən)

adverb

Many times; frequently.

☙ The contemporary pronunciation of *often* with a (t) is a classic example of a spelling pronunciation, in line with "boat-swain" for *bosun*, *comptroller* with an (mp) instead of an (n), and *falcon* pronounced with an (l).

But why shouldn't the *t* in *often* be pronounced? The answer lies in linguistic history. During the 16th and 17th centuries, English experienced a widespread loss of consonant sounds occurring in the middle of clusters, among them the (d) in *handsome* and *handkerchief,* the (p) in *raspberry,* and the (t) in *chestnut* and *often.*

Unfortunately, smart people couldn't leave well enough alone. To form a spelling pronunciation, you have to be educated—you have to know how to spell. Once people can read and spell, they notice the letters that nonliterate people never knew existed, and in some cases literate people feel obligated to pronounce silent letters that they notice. Such is the case with *often,* which is now commonly pronounced with the (t). Curiously, there are many other words with a written *t* in consonant clusters that have not been given spelling pronunciations. In *soften* and *listen,* for instance, the *t* generally remains silent.

[Middle English, alteration (probably influenced by *selden,* seldom) of *oft,* from Old English.]

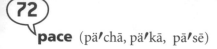

pace (pä′chā, pä′kā, pā′sē)

preposition

With the permission of; with deference to. Used to express polite or ironically polite disagreement: *I have not, pace my detractors, entered into any secret negotiations.*

Often italicized in writing as a foreign word to distinguish it from the verb *pace*, the preposition *pace* inevitably lends a very formal air to what is said. Properly used, *pace* means "with deference to; with the permission of," and it announces that you are about to give an opinion contrary to one held by a known person, and often an eminent one. In this way, it expresses polite (or ironically polite) disagreement. A more common and less erudite way of saying the same thing is *with all due respect to.* Here is an example of the use of *pace*: "*I had become bored with London society, which, pace Dr Johnson, is perfectly possible*" (Jane Stevenson, *Several Deceptions*). The word *pace* seems to hark back to an earlier era of oratory and formal debate, though it is still common in academic prose.

Pace comes from the Latin expression *pāce,* meaning "with all due respect to," and always has two syllables. There are three ways of pronouncing this word, (pä′chā), (pä′kā), and (pā′sē), and these pronunciations reflect three different traditions of pronouncing Latin words and phrases by English speakers.

In the one tradition, the letters of Latin words are pronounced much as they would be according to the rules of English spelling—except that a final *e* is not silent. This way of pronouncing Latin descends from the way Latin was pronounced by English scholars, lawyers, physicians, and clerics during the Middle Ages. (At the time, every country in Europe had its own way of pronouncing Latin as if it were the local language—a Spaniard would pronounce it like Spanish, a Frenchman like French, and an Italian like Italian.) According to this English tradition, *pace* is pronounced (pā′sē) and rhymes with *racy.* This old way of pronouncing Latin in English can be heard in other common words and phrases, such as the legal term *habeas corpus* (hā′bē-əs kôr′pəs), not (hä′bā-äs kōr′-po͞os), and the motto *e pluribus unum,* with *e* usually pronounced (ē), not (ā).

Another way of pronouncing *pace* reflects the pronunciation of Latin now common among members of the Roman Catholic Church when saying prayers or singing music in Latin. In this tradition, Latin words are read as they would be in Italian. (This is in fact just the national tradition of pronouncing Latin in Italy, as mentioned above, but the Church encouraged it in other countries as a way of unifying her followers.) In Italian, the letter *c* is pronounced (ch) before *e* or *i,* and so *pace* is pronounced (pä′chā) according to this tradition.

Since the 19th century, scholars have promoted a third tradition, in which Latin is pronounced approximately the way it was by Romans in Julius Caesar's day. During the golden age of Latin literature, Romans pronounced *c* before *e* as (k), and so Latin *pāce* was pronounced (pä′kā). Nowadays, when Latin is taught in English-speaking countries, students often learn to pronounce Latin according to this classical model. Some people may choose to pronounce *pace* as (pä′kā) in English because they wish to remain as faithful as possible to Latin as the Romans spoke it.

In this way, none of the three pronunciations of *pace* can really be considered incorrect, but (pā′sē) is probably the pronunciation that has been used in English-speaking countries the longest.

[Latin *pāce,* with all due respect to (used in such phrases as *pāce tua,* with all respect due to you, by your leave), from ablative case of *pāx,* peace.]

pastoral (păs′tə-rəl, pă-stôr′rəl)

adjective

1. Of, relating to, or portraying shepherds or rural life.
2. Of or relating to a pastor or the duties of a pastor: *pastoral duties; a pastoral letter.*

It is hard to say why people are tempted to pronounce *pastoral* with stress on the *–stor–*. After all, everyone knows how to pronounce the noun *pastor,* from which *pastoral* derives. Perhaps some people are misled by the similarity of *pastoral* to such words as *oral, floral,* and *amoral,* all of which are stressed on the second-to-last syllable. Perhaps others are led astray by the shifting of accent that occurs between the nouns *ancestor, funeral,* and *ornament* and the adjectives *ancestral, funereal,* and *ornamental.* But the traditional and more widely accepted pronunciation of *pastoral* is the one that places the stress squarely on the first syllable, as in *pastor.*

[Middle English, from Old French, from Latin *pāstōrālis,* from *pāstor,* shepherd.]

patina (păt′n-ə, pə-tē′nə)

noun

1. A thin greenish layer, usually basic copper sulfate, that forms on copper or copper alloys, such as bronze, as a result of corrosion. **2.** The sheen on a surface, especially one made of wood, produced by age or use. **3.** An appearance or change produced by behavior, practice, or use: *"People said afterward that they'd had no idea that beneath the fourth-grade patina of obedience and good manners I could be such a surprisingly irresponsible, daydreaming child"* (Philip Roth, *The Plot Against America*).

Though most words in Italian are stressed on the second-to-last syllable, there are many exceptions to this rule. The Italian word *patina* is one of them, and when it was borrowed into English it retained its original stress pattern, with emphasis on the first syllable, not on the second as in *cantina, fontina,* or *sestina,* all of which also derive from Italian. This remains its preferred pronunciation in Britain and among scrupulous speakers of English in the US, though the pronunciation (pə-tē′nə), rhyming with *Christina,* has become so widespread as to be completely acceptable and is even listed first in some dictionaries.

[Italian, from Latin, plate (from the incrustation on ancient metal plates and dishes), from Greek *patanē.*]

The first word of **piña colada** is often pronounced (pēn′ə), as if it were spelled "pina," without the tilde. This pronunciation is generally accepted by Anglophone Americans, but if you find yourself in a Spanish-speaking area and you feel the desire for a refreshing mixed drink, you might do well to ask for a **piña** ("peenya") **colada**.

piña colada (pēn′yə kō-lä′də, pēn′ə kō-lä′də,
   pĭn′yə kō-lä′də)

noun

A mixed drink made of rum, coconut cream, and unsweetened pineapple juice.

English is, as a written language, remarkably free of diacritics—those marks, like the German umlaut (¨) or the French acute accent (′), that help indicate a special phonetic value or distinguish words that are otherwise graphically identical. Other than the very rare and fairly old-fashioned use of the dieresis to indicate that two consecutive vowels are to be pronounced separately (as in *coöperate*) and the traditional use of an accent mark in poetry (as in *lovèd,* where it indicates that the *–ed* is to be pronounced as a separate syllable), English uses diacritics only in words that are relatively recent imports from other languages. Native speakers of English, in writing such words, often omit the diacritics altogether, turning *fiancée* into *fiancee* and *smörgåsbord* into *smorgasbord.* We also have a tendency to ignore unfamiliar diacritics in pronunciation. After all, how many native English speakers have any idea how the Swedish *å* properly ought to be pronounced?

Thus the first word of *piña colada* is often pronounced (pēn′ə), as if it were spelled "pina," without the tilde. This pronunciation is generally accepted by Anglophone Americans, but if you find yourself in a Spanish-speaking area and you feel the desire for a refreshing mixed drink, you might do well to ask for a *piña* ("peenya") *colada.*

[Spanish, strained pineapple : *piña,* pineapple (from Old Spanish *piña,* pinecone, from Latin *pīnea,* from *pīnus,* pine) + *colada,* strained, feminine past participle of *colar,* to strain (from Old Spanish, from Latin *colāre*).]

76

plethora (plĕth′ər-ə)

noun

An abundance or excess of something: *"his lights-out two-seamer sinker that clocks in the low nineties with late movement, resulting in a plethora of weakly hit ground-balls"* (Buzz Bissinger, *Three Nights in August*).

🐟 The proper pronunciation of *plethora* places the stress squarely on the *pleth–*. As with *remora* (the fish that attaches itself to the body of a swimming shark), many speakers who are unfamiliar with the correct pronunciation place the stress on the second syllable, as if it rhymed with *aurora* or *fedora*, but this pronunciation is regarded as incorrect by educated speakers, and it is not generally countenanced by the major dictionaries.

[Late Latin *plēthōra,* from Greek, from *plēthein,* to be full.]

77

portentous (pôr-tĕn′təs)

adjective

1. Of the nature of or constituting a portent; foreboding: *"the Hessian marauders, the threat of whose coming had long hung like a portentous cloud over the Berkshire valley"* (Edward Bellamy, *The Duke of Stockbridge*). **2.** Full of unspecifiable significance; exciting wonder and awe: *"Such a portentous and mysterious monster roused all my curiosity"* (Herman Melville, *Moby Dick*).

🐟 The usual pronunciation of this word is (pôr-tĕn′təs). However, under the influence of words like *contentious, pretentious,* and *sententious, portentous* is sometimes pronounced (pôr-tĕn′-shəs), as if it were spelled *portentious.* Neither the pronunciation ending in (shəs) nor the spelling ending in *–tious* (which crops up occasionally in print) is considered standard.

[From Old French *portentueux, portenteux,* and Latin *portentuōsus, portentōsus* (French, from Latin), from Latin *portentum,* portent, from neuter past participle of *portendere,* to portend : *por-,* forth, forward + *tendere,* to hold (something) out, offer.]

78

potash (pŏt′ăsh′)

noun

Any of several compounds containing potassium, used chiefly in making glass, soaps, and fertilizers.

🐚 If you know anything at all about potash, you know that it is a chemical compound with various industrial uses. In fact, the word *potash* can refer to any of several compounds, all of which contain potassium. But how is *potash* pronounced? The language of chemistry is part of the language of science, and the language of science constructs many of its terms from foreign roots or from preexisting foreign words. Especially common sources are Greek and Latin (as in *amniocentesis, meson,* and *xerothermic*). English also derives a sizable number of scientific words from Arabic (such as *algorithm* and *Betelgeuse*). But *potash* is not so exotic, and it is deceptively simple to pronounce. Though it is related to the older Dutch word *potaschen, potash* itself is a simple English compound made up of the humdrum nouns *pot* and *ash;* like most compounds in English, its pronunciation is simply the sum of its constituent parts, with a slightly stronger stress on the first element.

[From the fact that this substance was originally obtained by leaching wood ashes and evaporating the leach in a pot.]

primer (prĭm′ər)

noun

1. An elementary textbook for teaching children to read. **2.** A book that covers the basic elements of a subject.

🖎 *Primer* (meaning the stuff you apply to a surface before painting it) and *primer* (meaning a textbook covering the basic elements of a subject) are what one might call etymological cousins, both being derived ultimately from the Latin *prīmus*, "first." But they are not siblings, much less identical twins. The first *primer* is simply "something that primes" and is a compound of the verb *prime,* "to prepare," with the suffix *–er.* This *primer* is thus pronounced with the same (ī) vowel that appears in the verb *prime.* The verb *prime* comes from the adjective *prime,* "first," and this adjective comes from Latin *prīmus.* The textbook *primer* comes from *prīmus* via the Medieval Latin *prīmārium,* "prayer book for laypeople, devotional manual." Since it is not descended from English *prime*, it is not surprising that its pronunciation has a different vowel sound—not the (ī) of *prime* but the (ĭ) of *prim.*

[Middle English, devotional manual, from Norman French, from Medieval Latin *prīmārium,* from neuter of *prīmārius,* first, from Latin, from *prīmus,* first.]

processes (prŏs′ĕs-ĭz, prō′sĕs-ĭz, prŏs′ĭs-sēz′,
    prō′sĭs-sēz′)

noun

Plural of **process**. A series of actions, changes, or
functions that bring about a result.

℘ In American English, the word *process* is usually pronounced
with a short *o* as (prŏs′ĕs), in a similar fashion to the noun
progress.

In recent years there has been a tendency to pronounce the
plural *processes* as (prŏs′ĭs-sēz′), with a long *e* as in *me* in the last
syllable, rather than the short *i* as in *pit* that you would expect in
an English word and that you hear in the word *premises.* The
long *e* pronunciation of the plural may have arisen by analogy
with the plurals of certain words of Greek origin, such as *analy-
sis* and *neurosis.* But since *process* does not come from Greek,
there seems little reason to pronounce its plural as if it did.

Nonetheless, this pronunciation occurs with some frequency
even in the speech of more educated Americans. It is generally
considered an acceptable variant, although it may strike some
listeners as a tad pretentious.

The pronunciation of *process* and its plural with a long *o,* as
(prō′sĕs), is widely used in British and Canadian English and
may sound a bit peculiar to American ears. But it is not stigmatized and is listed as standard in most dictionaries.

[Middle English *proces*, from Old French, development,
from Latin *prōcessus*, forward movement, from *prōcēdere*, to
move forward : *prō-*, forward + *cēdere*, to go.]

puerile (pyŏo′ər-əl, pyŏor′əl, pyŏo′ər-īl′, pyŏor′īl′, pwĕr′əl, pwĕr′īl′)

adjective

1. Belonging to childhood; juvenile. **2.** Immature; childish.

🌿 Few English words start with *puer–*. Most of the *puer–* words are medical terms that laypeople are unlikely to hear spoken, such as *puerperal* or *puerperium*. Some geographic names, such as *Puerto Vallarta* and *Puerto Rico*, also begin with *puer–*. So how should you pronounce *puerile*?

Both the beginning and the end of the word present challenges. It is standard to pronounce the first part either as (pyŏo′ər-), rhyming with *fewer*, or as (pyŏor-), sounding like *pure*, though this distinction might not be meaningful to speakers in certain parts of the country because of regional variation of the *u* vowel before *r*. Another variant pronunciation is (pwĕr-), similar to the Spanish pronunciation of the first part of *Puerto Rico*. This is probably a spelling pronunciation, and it has become very common recently, but it has not—or not yet anyway—been listed in dictionaries as acceptable. Pronouncing the first part of *puerile* as (pôr-), the way many English speakers say the opening syllable of *Puerto Rico* (as if it was "Porto Rico") is simply wrong.

The second part of the word is not stressed and is usually pronounced with the "uh" sound known as *schwa*, so that the word can rhyme with *mural*. A variant with a long *i* in the second syllable, rhyming with *aisle,* is also acceptable.

[Latin *puerīlis,* from *puer,* child, boy.]

---

quay (kē, kā)

noun

A wharf or reinforced bank where ships are loaded or unloaded.

🖎 *Quay* was borrowed into English from French in the 14th century and was spelled both *keye* and *kaye* in the centuries that followed, suggesting that its pronunciation was somewhat variable (as it is today). The *qu–* spelling was introduced, again by influence of French, in the 18th century and eventually won out as the standard spelling.

The word is usually pronounced to rhyme with *key,* but the pronunciation rhyming with *day* has never gone away and is now considered standard as well. It may also show some influence of the word *cay*, which refers to a small sandy island and came into English from the native Caribbean language Taíno via Spanish *cayo.*

The further spelling pronunciation (kwā), in which the letters *qu* are rendered as (kw), is also listed in some dictionaries but may strike some listeners as uninformed.

[Middle English *keye,* from Old North French *cai,* of Celtic origin.]

quietus (kwī-ē′təs)

noun

1. Something that serves to suppress, check, or eliminate: *"It put the quietus on Dolores's and my friendship"* (Marge Piercy, *Sleeping with Cats: A Memoir*). **2.** Release from life; death. **3.** A final discharge, as of a duty or debt.

☙ In his famous speech, Shakespeare's character Hamlet asks why people decide to continue living in the face of unbearable pain and insurmountable obstacles. He asks why a person does not take his own life "When he himself might his quietus make / With a bare bodkin" (that is, when he himself might end his life with a simple knife). For readers who have seen *quietus* in print but have never heard the word in conversation, Hamlet's pronunciation of it (as interpreted by any decent Shakespearean actor) may give us pause. In writing, *quietus* would seem to contain the word *quiet*—and in fact, both words derive from the Latin *quiētus*—but the two words are stressed on different syllables. *Quiet* is, of course, pronounced with stress on its first syllable. *Quietus* is stressed on its second syllable. This pronunciation is essential to preserve Shakespeare's poetic meter—the regular pattern of emphasis—in Hamlet's line of iambic pentameter: "When HE himSELF might HIS quiEtus MAKE." Along with the difference in emphasis comes a difference in vowel quality—the *e* of *quietus* is a long *e*, making it rhyme with "greet us."

[Short for Middle English *quietus (est),* (he is) discharged (of an obligation), from Medieval Latin *quiētus (est),* from Latin, (he is) at rest.]

reprise (rĭ-prēz′)

noun

1. *Music* **a.** A repetition of a phrase or verse. **b.** A return to an original theme. **2.** A recurrence or resumption of an action.

☙ In its musical (and most common) use meaning "a repetition of a phrase or verse" or "a return to an original theme," *reprise* is traditionally pronounced (rĭ-prēz′), with its last syllable rhyming with *freeze*. This reflects the influence of French when the musical use of the word was adopted in the 18th century. The word has other, older uses in law, and the pronunciation of these uses as (rĭ-prīz′) with a long *i* sound, as in *pie*, reflects the older history of the word, going back to the Middle Ages. This long *i* pronunciation is sometimes used in musical contexts, where it is often considered a mistake. It arose either as a spelling pronunciation (by people with limited musical exposure) or by influence of the related word *reprisal*, which has a long *i* in its stressed syllable.

[Middle English, act of taking back, from Old French, from feminine past participle of *reprendre,* to take back, from Latin *reprendere, reprehendere* : *re-*, again + *prehendere,* to seize.]

respite (rĕs′pĭt)

noun

A usually short interval of rest or relief.

⚘ Though *respite* is spelled very much like *despite,* the two words are pronounced quite differently, even though they both found their way to Modern English by more or less the same etymological route, from Latin, by way of Old French and Middle English. Rather than being pronounced with stress on the second syllable and with a long *i* sound as *despite* is, *respite* is properly pronounced with stress on the first syllable and with a short *i* sound as in *pit*—so short, in fact, that in everyday speech the vowel of the second syllable approaches the schwa sound (ə), as if *respite* rhymed with *despot.*

The word *respite* thus stands as an exception to one of the most generally applicable rules of thumb for English pronunciation: that words with similar spellings and similar pedigrees are usually pronounced similarly.

[Middle English, from Old French *respit,* from Latin *respectus,* refuge, looking back, from *respicere,* to look back at, regard : *re-*, back + *specere,* to look at.]

ribald (rĭb′əld, rī′bôld′)

adjective

Characterized by or indulging in vulgar, lewd humor.

🖎 *Ribald* contains no roots, prefixes, or suffixes that you are likely to recognize. It exists in a vacuum, as it were, bearing no obvious relation to any other English words except its own derivatives such as *ribaldry*. Even its language of origin (French) is not particularly evident in its spelling, which has undergone a change in the eight centuries or so since it was adopted into English. When forced to guess how to pronounce *ribald*, some people who are unfamiliar with the word seize on the visual similarity of *ribald* to *rib* and pronounce *ribald* to rhyme with *dribbled*. Others, distracted by the *–bald*, pronounce it as if it rhymed with *piebald*. The first of these two pronunciations is the traditionally correct one, though the *rib–* of *ribald* actually has nothing to do with skeletal anatomy. You may find it easy to remember the correct pronunciation if you keep in mind that both *ribaldry* and *ribbing* are forms of joking around, though the similarities between the two words are, as it were, only skin deep and do not extend down to their etymological bones.

[From Middle English *ribaud,* ribald person, from Old French, from *riber,* to be wanton, from Middle High German, *rīban,* to rub, be in heat, copulate, from Old High German.]

salve (săv, säv)

noun

1. An analgesic or medicinal ointment. **2.** Something that soothes or consoles; a balm.

transitive verb
> Past participle and past tense: **salved**
> Present participle: **salving**
> Third person singular present tense: **salves**

1. To soothe or heal with salve. **2.** To ease the distress or agitation of (a person or a person's feelings); assuage: *I salved my conscience by apologizing.*

☙ Of the few *–alve* words in English, several—*calve, halve,* and *salve*—are typically pronounced with a silent *l*. These words, in the same process of language change that affected *almond*, all lost their (l) sound sometime around the 16th century. Only *valve* and its derivatives such as *bivalve* and *trivalve* normally retain the (l) sound in pronunciation. For most English speakers, *half* and *calf* are such familiar words that we never notice the fact that the *l* is silent when we say them. *Salve*, though, is less common, and it is similar in spelling to *solve* and *salvation*, both of which (like *salve*) have to do with fixing, healing, or saving and both of which are pronounced with the *l* spoken rather than silent. This is probably why some speakers pronounce the *l* in *salve* even though they omit it in *calve* and *halve*. It may also explain why even those speakers who do omit the *l* are torn between saying (săv), the traditional pronunciation, rhyming with *calve* and *halve*, and säv, rhyming with *suave*, which is for most Americans identical to the (ŏ) or (ô) vowel sound in *solve*.

[Middle English, from Old English *sealf*.]

88
schism (skĭz′əm, sĭz′əm)

noun

1. A separation or division into factions. **2.** A formal breach of union within a Christian church.

🙟 This word, which was originally spelled *scisme, cisme,* and *sisme* in English, is traditionally pronounced (sĭz′əm), without a (k) sound. The modern spelling with the *h* dates back to the 16th century, when the word was respelled to resemble its Latin and Greek ancestors. The pronunciation with (k), (skĭz′əm), was long regarded as incorrect, but it became so common in both British and American English that it gained acceptability and now predominates in standard American usage.

    Some people say (shĭz′əm), with an initial (sh), but they are a small minority, and this pronunciation cannot be considered standard.

[Middle English *scisme,* from Old French, from Latin *schisma,* from Greek *skhisma,* from *skhizein,* to split.]

89
sherbet (shûr′bĭt)

noun

A frozen dessert made primarily of fruit juice, sugar, and water, and also containing milk, egg white, or gelatin.

🙟 The "sherbert" spelling of *sherbet* is rare in printed sources, and it has no etymological justification. No *r* appears in the second syllables of the Turkish, Persian, and Arabic words from which *sherbet* ultimately derives. But in English, the insertion of an (r) sound in the second syllable of *sherbet* is extremely common. Many speakers will pronounce this word with a second (r) even when reading aloud from a menu or a package that uses the historically correct *r*-less spelling.

However, in the US the past few decades have seen an explosion in the popularity of sherbet's close cousin *sorbet* (which is often though not always pronounced in the French manner, rhyming with *café*). Whether the trendiness of sorbet will have any lasting effect on the pronunciation of *sherbet*—for instance, by weaning people away from the "sherbert" pronunciation—remains to be seen.

[From Ottoman Turkish, sweet fruit drink, from Persian *sharbat*, from Arabic *šarba*, drink, from *šariba*, to drink.]

(90)

sloth (slôth, slōth, slŏth)

noun

1. Aversion to work or exertion; laziness; indolence. **2.** Any of various slow-moving, arboreal, edentate mammals of the family Bradypodidae of South and Central America, having long hooklike claws by which they hang upside down from tree branches and feeding on leaves, buds, and fruits.

🐾 This word is a noun formed in medieval times from the adjective *slow* with a *–th* suffix added on. Not surprisingly, the traditional (and British) pronunciation rhymes with *both* and *growth*. But Americans usually pronounce this word to fit the short *o* pattern of *broth*, *cloth*, and *moth*. This pronunciation is especially prevalent when reference is made to those slow-moving animals, the two-toed and three-toed sloths.

[Middle English *slowth*, from *slow*, slow, from Old English *slāw*.]

stigmata (stĭg-mä′tə, stĭg-măt′ə, stĭg′mə-tə)

noun

A plural of **stigma**. **1.** A mark, spot, or scar. **2.** The sticky tip of a flower pistil, on which pollen is deposited. **3.** An attitude of shame or disgrace that is associated with something: *There should be no stigma attached to doing strenuous physical work.*

❧ *Stigmata* is a plural of the word *stigma,* which also has a regular plural form *stigmas.* These days the *stigmata* plural, which comes from Latin, is largely limited to religious contexts, referring to the marks corresponding to the wounds of the crucified Jesus believed to be given by God to certain extraordinarily devout people. Everyone knows that *stigma* and *stigmatize* are pronounced with stress on the *stig–,* and nearly everyone knows that *astigmatism* is stressed on *–stig–* as well. The traditional pronunciation of *stigmata,* too, puts stress on the *stig–.* Where, then, did the (stĭg-mä′tə) pronunciation, with its stress on the *–ma–,* come from? Most likely it arose out of a vague awareness of the fact that words ending in *a* are often borrowed from languages such as Spanish and Italian, and that in such words the stress is typically on the second-to-last syllable—as in *chinchilla, fermata, mascara, regatta,* or *vendetta.* Or perhaps the pronunciation was also influenced by such words of Latin origin as *errata* and *desiderata,* which are often pronounced (ĭ-rä′tə) and (dĭ-sĭd′-ə-rä′tə), in English. In the Latin originals of these words, the stress falls on the *a* preceding the *t.* The pronunciation of *stigmata* with stress on the *–ma–* may not be historically correct, but it is so widespread as to be universally acceptable; one might say that it bears no social stigma.

[Latin *stigma, stigmat-,* tattoo indicating slave or criminal status, from Greek, tattoo mark, from *stizein, stig-,* to prick.]

strophe (strō′fē)

noun

A stanza of a poem, especially one made up of lines of varying length.

🐾 There is a general rule in English that an *e* is usually silent when it appears at the end of a word and immediately following a consonant (or a pair of consonants). Examples of this rule include *bribe, divorce, theme, wage, matte,* and so on. But foreign words borrowed into English are less likely than native words to follow this rule—as in the cases of the German *schadenfreude,* the Japanese *kamikaze,* the Italian *penne,* or the Hawaiian *nene.* The word *strophe,* like other originally Greek words such as *calliope, epitome,* and *hyperbole,* is properly pronounced with a long *e* as in *me* at the end.

[Greek *strophē*, a turning, stanza, from *strephein*, to turn.]

timbre (tăm′bər, tĭm′bər)

noun

The combination of qualities of a sound that distinguishes it from other sounds of the same pitch and volume.

☙ The word *timbre* is very useful, even for those of us without any particular interest or technical training in music or acoustics. No other word so accurately denotes the quality that distinguishes the sound of a flute from that of a trumpet, or the sound of a woman's voice from that of a man speaking in falsetto. Laypeople sometimes use the word *tone* to indicate this distinctive quality of a sound, but *tone* can also refer to volume (as in *people speaking in hushed tones*) or to the pitch of sounds (as in *Mandarin Chinese uses four basic tones*). Perhaps if people were less uncertain about its pronunciation, they would be more likely to use the word *timbre*, and our discussions about sound would have greater precision. Though many dictionaries, including the *American Heritage*, grudgingly accept a pronunciation of *timbre* that makes it sound like *timber*, all dictionaries and most musicians prefer a pronunciation that is somewhat closer to the original French: (tăm′bər), rhyming with *amber*.

[French, from Old French, drum, clapperless bell, probably from Greek *tumpanon*, kettledrum.]

You should try to remember that, just as competitors in a triathlon move through each of the three events without stopping to rest, so should you move smoothly through each of **triathlon**'s three syllables, without allowing an intervening schwa to slacken your pace.

triathlon (trī-ăth′lən, trī-ăth′lŏn′)

noun

An athletic contest in which participants compete without stopping in three successive events, usually long-distance swimming, bicycling, and running.

🖎 The extra vowel that some people insert into their pronunciation of *triathlon* (and, to a lesser extent, *athlete*) is not that well understood. It is tempting to say that people pronounce *triathlon* as a four-syllable word (as if it were "triathalon") because of the inherent difficulty of pronouncing the consonant cluster –*thl*–. But on closer examination that seems not to be the case. Most speakers of English have absolutely no trouble pronouncing *Bethlehem, earthling, monthly, ruthless,* or *worthless,* all of which contain the same –*thl*– cluster. The more likely explanation, given the fact that a triathlon is an athletic event, is that people are inclined to make *triathlon* sound a bit more like *marathon* than it properly ought to. The same mispronunciation also crops up in *biathlon, pentathlon,* and *decathlon*—but less frequently, because those events are less well known among non-athletes and perhaps also because the long-distance running component of the triathlon more closely resembles (and sometimes in fact amounts to) a marathon. In any case, you should try to remember that, just as competitors in a triathlon move through each of the three events without stopping to rest, so should you move smoothly through each of *triathlon*'s three syllables, without allowing an intervening schwa to slacken your pace.

[*tri-*, three (from Greek and Latin *tri-*) + -*athlon,* as in English *pentathlon* (from Greek *pentāthlon : penta-,* five + *āthlon,* prize).]

Uranus (yŏŏr′ə-nəs, yŏŏ-rā′nəs)

noun

1. *Greek Mythology* The earliest supreme god, a person-ification of the sky, who was the son and consort of Gaea and the father of the Cyclopes and Titans. **2.** The seventh planet from the sun, revolving about it every 84.01 years at a mean distance of approximately 2.9 billion kilometers (1.8 billion miles), having a mean equatorial diameter of 51,118 kilometers (31,764 miles) and a mass 14.6 times that of Earth.

℘ One standard pronunciation of *Uranus* puts the stress on the first syllable and reduces the second syllable to a schwa sound. This pronunciation also has the advantage of being marginally less likely to provoke giggles if you use it in the presence of twelve-year-olds—or adults with the mentality of twelve-year-olds, for that matter. If you do use it, and if any listeners object that your pronunciation sounds odd to them, you can simply inform them that it is historically correct and that it preserves the pattern of emphasis in the Late Latin word *Ūranus*. If the skeptics remain unconvinced, simply reply that the first-syllable stress on *Uranus* also reflects the usage of the majority of astronomers.

[Late Latin *Ūranus,* from Greek *ouranos,* heaven, the god Uranus.]

victual (vĭt′l)

noun

1. Food fit for human consumption. **2. victuals** Food supplies; provisions.

🐚 Should you be served if you ask at a motel restaurant for some "vick-too-uhls"?

This word is properly pronounced (vĭt′l), with two syllables and no (k) sound. It was borrowed back in the 14th century from the Old French form *vitaille*, which had stress and a diphthong in the second syllable, but the word was Anglicized after that to put the stress up front in the manner of most native English words.

The spelling with *c* (and a little later with *u*) has a long history too, in both French and English. This spelling is a learned one, showing off the knowledge that the word came from Late Latin *victuālia*, "provisions."

The word is now usually spelled *victual*, or on occasion *vittle*, but the pronunciation has remained (vĭt′l).

[Alteration (influenced by Late Latin *vīctuālia*, provisions) of Middle English *vitaille*, from Old French, from Late Latin *vīctuālia*, provisions, from neuter plural of Latin *vīctuālis*, of nourishment, from *vīctus*, nourishment, from past participle of *vīvere*, to live.]

viscount (vī′kount′)

noun

1. A nobleman ranking below an earl or count and above a baron. **2.** Used as a title for such a nobleman.

🐾 The –*count* of *viscount* presents no difficulty for a reader unfamiliar with the word's pronunciation. And the prefix *vis*– is, as one might guess, related to the *vice* of *vice admiral, vicegerent,* and *vice president.* The pronunciation of *viscount* may surprise you, however. You may suppose that because the British—and many Americans—say the word *marquis* with a spoken *s,* the *s* in *viscount* is pronounced as well. There is, indeed, some justification for such an assumption. After all, both words denote ranks of nobility, both have come to us from Old French via Middle English, and in both words the *s* follows an *i.* But, in fact, the *s* of *viscount* is silent. In both British and American English, this word is properly pronounced vī′kount′ ("viecount").

[Middle English, from Old French *visconte,* from Medieval Latin *vicecomes, vicecomit-* : Late Latin *vice-,* deputy , vice-, + Late Latin *comes,* occupant of any state office, from Latin, companion.]

wont (wônt, wōnt, wŭnt)

adjective

1. Accustomed or used: *"Instead of being a rationale for state-sponsored violence, as its critics are wont to say today, the theory is a rather desperate effort to curtail it"* (James Carroll, *Constantine's Sword*). **2.** Likely: *"Bread … I baked before my fire … but it was wont to get smoked and to have a piney flavor"* (Henry David Thoreau, *Walden*).

noun

Customary practice; usage: *"Snyder, as was his wont, tried to accentuate the positive"* (Jeremy Schaap, *Triumph*).

🖎 The most traditionally correct pronunciations of *wont* are (wōnt), the common pronunciation in Britain, sounding like the contraction *won't*, and (wŭnt), the historic American pronunciation, rhyming with *hunt*. However, the most common form of *wont* in contemporary American speech is probably (wônt), which to most people's ears sounds similar to (or even identical with) the word *want*. This (wônt) pronunciation may in fact be motivated by a confusion of the meanings of *wont* and *want*, both of which have to do with personal inclination. Whichever pronunciation of *wont* you use, you can rest assured that you have at least some dictionaries on your side—but you can be certain you *won't* please those whose *wonted* pronunciation of *wont* differs from yours.

[Middle English, past participle of *wonen*, to dwell, remain, be accustomed to, from Old English *wunian*.]

Xhosa (kō′sä, kō′zə)

noun
   Plural: **Xhosa** *or* **Xhosas**

1. A member of a Bantu people inhabiting the eastern part of Cape Province, South Africa. **2.** The Nguni language of this people, closely related to Zulu.

The correct Xhosa pronunciation of *Xhosa* begins with a lateral click—a sound that exists only in certain African languages. This click is not an inherently difficult sound to make, but the mechanism of clicking is very unlike the ways speech sounds are produced in English—it depends on using the tongue to quickly suck air in through the sides of the mouth, rather than holding air or letting it out as in all native English speech sounds. Consequently, English speakers find it very difficult to incorporate the click smoothly into their pronunciation of words like *Xhosa*. English has therefore adopted the (k) sound as an acceptable (if imperfect) approximation of the Xhosa *x*.

   A complicating factor is the *h* that follows the *x* in *Xhosa*. Simple *x* represents the lateral click pronounced without a following puff of air, while *xh* represents the click with a following puff of air.

[Xhosa -*Xhosa*, as in *amaXhosa*, the Xhosa people, and *isiXhosa*, the Xhosa language.]

ye (*th*ē, yē)

definite article

Archaic The.

In an attempt to seem quaint or old-fashioned, many store signs such as "Ye Olde Coffee Shoppe" use spellings that are no longer current. The word *ye* in such signs looks identical to the archaic second-person plural pronoun *ye,* but it is in fact not the same word. *Ye* in "Ye Olde Coffee Shoppe" is just an older spelling of the definite article *the.* The *y* in this *ye* was never pronounced (y) but was rather the result of improvisation by early printers. In Old English and early Middle English, the sound (*th*) was represented by the letter thorn (þ). When printing presses were first set up in England in the 1470s, the type came from Continental Europe, where this letter was not in use. The letter *y* was used instead because in the handwriting of the day the loop of the letter thorn was often not connected to the upright, and so the thorn looked very similar to *y.* So spellings like *ye* for *the,* and *yt* or *yat* for *that* were not only common but survived into the 19th century.

However, the modern revival of this archaic form of *the* has not been accompanied by a revival of the knowledge of how it was pronounced, with the result that (yē) is the usual pronunciation today.

[Misreading of *ye,* from Middle English *þe,* alternate spelling of *the,* the (using the letter thorn þ).]

The 100 Words

acumen
aegis
affluent
almond
antipodes
asphalt
babel
banal
boatswain
cache
cacophony
cadre
Celtic
chaise longue
chiaroscuro
chicanery
chimera
chutzpah
claddagh
coccyx
coitus
comptroller
conch
concupiscence
coup de grâce
covert
cumin
daiquiri
debacle
desuetude
desultory
detritus
Diaspora
divisive

dour
elegiac
epitome
epoch
err
feng shui
flaccid
forbade
forte
geisha
genre
gnocchi
gyro
Halley's comet
harass
hegemony
hovel
impious
jejune
kiln
kudos
lingerie
loath
long-lived
machination
maraschino
marquis
metastasize
mischievous
moot
mores
Neanderthal
niche
nuclear

oblique
oeuvre
often
pace
pastoral
patina
piña colada
plethora
portentous
potash
primer
processes
puerile
quay
quietus
reprise
respite
ribald
salve
schism
sherbet
sloth
stigmata
strophe
timbre
triathlon
Uranus
victual
viscount
wont
Xhosa
ye